Your New Life

Eleventh Edition

by L. Jeter Walker

AN INDEPENDENT-STUDY TEXTBOOK

Developed in cooperation with Global University staff

Address of the Global University office in your area:

What is new in this printing:

- Unit evaluation answer keys are now located at the back of this textbook for self-evaluation. Unit evaluations are no longer submitted for credit.
- Students must apply and enroll at http://sed.globalutraining.com and complete the online final examination to receive credit.
- Students may also e-mail sed@globaluniversity.edu to find an office in their country for enrollment.

School for Evangelism and Discipleship
Global University
1211 South Glenstone
Springfield, MO 65804
USA

© 1969, 1974, 1979, 1980, 1986, 1990, 1991, 1992, 1993, 2004, 2007
Global University
All rights reserved. First edition 1969.
Eleventh edition 2007.

Unless otherwise indicated, Scripture quotations are from The Holy Bible, New International Version®. NIV®. Copyright © 1973, 1978, 1984 by Biblica. Used by permission. All rights reserved.

PN 11.15.01

ISBN 978-0-7617-1229-9

www.globaluniversity.edu
www.globalreach.org

Printed in the United States of America by Gospel Publishing House, Springfield, Missouri.

Table of Contents

PREFACE 5
THE CHRISTIAN LIFE SERIES 7
ABOUT THE AUTHOR 13

UNIT ONE

   1   You Have Begun a New Life 16
   2   You Are Learning to Walk 26
   3   Your Father Is Speaking to You 38
   4   Do You Want to Grow? 50
   5   New Life, New Activities 60

UNIT TWO

   6   Your New Standards 76
   7   You Have a Helper 84
   8   Your Life Is a Light 94
   9   How to Have a Happy Home 106
  10   Your New Freedom 118

UNIT EVALUATIONS 133
UNIT EVALUATION ANSWER KEY 141
STUDENT QUESTIONNAIRE 145
FINAL EXAM INSTRUCTIONS 149

Christian Life Series

Your New Life
Your Bible
Who Jesus Is
The Church
Personal Evangelism
Bible Ethics
When You Pray
How to Study the Bible
Your Helpful Friend
Christian Worship
Christian Workers
Marriage and the Home
God's Design—Your Choice
John's Gospel
We Believe
What Churches Do
The Teaching Ministry
The Christian in the Community

PREFACE

When you asked Jesus Christ to be your Savior, a wonderful event took place. You were brought out of darkness into light. Your sins were forgiven, and you were born into the family of God. You received a new life. This book is about the new life you now have because of what Jesus did for you.

Your new life is a gift directly from your heavenly Father. It will last forever! Though it comes from God in heaven, you begin to live it now on earth. Day by day, you will be changed by God's power until you become more like Him. Your old desires and habits will fall away as you obey Him. New, beautiful patterns will form.

Just how does all this happen? What can you expect now that you belong to God? What differences will there be? How does your heavenly Father want you to live? How does He tell you what He wants you to do? What kind of help does He give you? This course was written to answer these questions. You will discover important truths about the life God has given to you.

Your New Life

Introduction 7

THE CHRISTIAN LIFE SERIES

Your New Life is one of eighteen courses in this practical discipleship program for new believers. The Christian Life Series is a study to help students grow in their relationship with Christ, interact with the Word of God, and better understand God's purposes for their lives.

Students will study basic Christian topics under six reoccurring themes. The courses are conversational in style and easy to read. The following chart illustrates how the units of study are organized for the Christian Life Series.

	Unit One	Unit Two	Unit Three
Spiritual Life	Your New Life	When You Pray	God's Design—Your Choice
The Bible	Your Bible	How to Study the Bible	John's Gospel
Theology	Who Jesus Is	Your Helpful Friend	We Believe
The Church	The Church	Christian Worship	What Churches Do
Service	Personal Evangelism	Christian Workers	The Teaching Ministry
Christian Ethics	Bible Ethics	Marriage and the Home	The Christian in the Community

Before You Begin

For Official Credit and a Certificate

Students who are officially enrolled with Global University through the International office in Springfield, MO, USA and have paid the appropriate fees may earn an end of series **Christian Life Certificate** by completing all the course requirements including the final examination for each course and requesting a certificate. Students studying through a center or group should contact their instructor or director for information concerning a certificate.

- Students may officially enroll in the School for Evangelism and Discipleship (SED) courses online at **http://sed.globalutraining.com** or by contacting student services at Gloal University.

- To study and obtain a certificate in one of our offices worldwide please fill out the form located at http://www.globaluniversity.edu/request_info.cfm to determine if there is a study group in your country or area.

This material may be studied for personal enrichment without official enrollment, which does NOT award a transcript or certificate from resources such as www.globalreach.org or by purchasing the book from Global University (http://www.globaluniversity.edu/PDF/orderSED.pdf). However, we do ask those who take advantage of these resources to consider making a donation to the Global University Evangelism Fund or Project Timothy. Please visit www.globaluniversity.edu and click on "giving."

Ways to Study this Course

This course has been written so that you can study it by yourself. We like to say "the teacher is in the book." However, you may also study this course in various types of group settings. If you study this course by yourself, all of your work can be completed by following the instructions in this study guide. If you are studying in a study group, be sure to follow any additional directions your instructor may give.

Your church or group may partner with Global University to open a study group. Visit us online at www.globaluniversity.edu or contact the study group coordinator at Global University for more information.

How to Use this Book

How much time you actually need to study each lesson depends in part on your knowledge of the subject and the strength of your study skills before you begin the course. The time you spend also depends on the extent to which you follow directions and develop skills necessary for independent study. Plan your study schedule so that you spend enough time to reach the objectives stated by the author of the course and your personal objectives as well.

Each lesson includes an introduction, an outline and goals to guide your study, application study questions throughout the lesson, and answers to those questions at the end of each lesson so you may review your learning progress.

Suggestions for Studying

1. Set aside quiet and regular times for your study. It will be easier to concentrate if study is part of your daily habits.

2. Pray as you begin each study session. With an open Bible, the Holy Spirit, and this course, you are in the classroom of the Holy Spirit. Ask the Lord to help you understand the lesson and apply it to your life.

3. Read the lesson introduction, the lesson outline and goals. The lesson outline and goals will give you an overview of the subject, help you focus your attention on the most important points as you study, and tell you what you should learn.

4. Begin to carefully read the lesson. Look up Bible

references and take any notes that may be helpful. The Bible verses reinforce important points in the lesson.
5. Answer the application study questions in the spaces provided. Most of the questions in the lesson can be answered in spaces provided in this textbook. Longer answers should be written in a notebook or journal. As you write your answers, be sure to record the number and title of the lesson. **Do not look ahead at the answers** until you have written your answer. If you give your own answers, you will remember what you study much better. *After* you have answered the application questions, check your answers with those given at the end of the lesson. Then review those you did not answer correctly. The answers are not given in the usual numerical order so that you will not accidentally see the answer to the next question. These application questions are very important. They will help you remember the main ideas presented in the lesson and apply the principles you have learned.
6. At the end of each unit, answer the unit evaluation questions, then check your answers using the answer key provided. Review difficult questions.
7. Take your time and study at a comfortable pace.

How to Answer Study Questions

This course uses many different kinds of questions. Below are samples of the three most common types and how to answer them.

Multiple-Choice

A multiple-choice question asks you to choose an answer from the ones that are given.

Example

1 The Bible has a total of
 a) 100 books.
 b) 66 books.
 c) 27 books.

The correct answer is **b)** 66 books. You would make a circle around **b)** as shown above.

(For some multiple-choice items, more than one answer will be correct. In that case, you would circle the letter in front of each correct answer.)

True-False

A true-false question or item asks you to choose which of several statements are true.

Example

2   Which statements below are true?
   a) The Bible has a total of 120 books.
   (b) The Bible is a message for believers today.
   c) All of the Bible authors wrote in the Hebrew language.
   (d) The Holy Spirit inspired the writers of the Bible.

Statements **b)** and **d)** are true. You would make a circle around these two letters to show your choices, as you see above.

Matching

A matching question or item asks you to match things that go together, such as names with descriptions, or Bible books with their authors.

Example

3   Write the number for the leader's name in front of each phrase that describes something he did.
   ..*1*..**a)** Received the Law at Mt. Sinai   1) Moses
   ..*2*..**b)** Led the Israelites across the Jordan   2) Joshua
   ..*2*..**c)** Marched around Jericho
   ..*1*..**d)** Lived in Pharaoh's court

Phrases **a)** and **d)** refer to Moses, and phrases **b)** and **c)** refer to Joshua. You would write 1 beside **a)** and **d)**, and 2 beside **b)** and **c)**, as you see above.

Unit Evaluations and Final Examination

At the end of this course, you will find the unit evaluations. Unit evaluations are NO LONGER counted as part of your course grade. However, unit evaluation scores indicate how well you learned the material and how well you may do on the final examination. After completing each unit evaluation, check your answers with the answers provided at the end of this textbook. You can then review the information in your course text and Bible concerning questions that were difficult for you. Reviewing the goals, application questions and answers, and unit exams will help you to prepare for the final examination. If you are not studying officially with a Global University office or study group you will still benefit by completing the unit evaluations.

The instructions for taking the final examination are available online using your student login and password. The final examination is only required for officially enrolled students (http://sed.globalutraining.com). Students studying through a national office or local study group should contact their instructor or director for information concerning unit evaluations and the final examination.

Additional Helps

For more information concerning our course content, purchases, and the SED Study Group Manual, please visit http://www.globaluniversity.edu/studygroups_forms.cfm.

Also visit us at www.globalreach.org for additional resources.

ABOUT THE AUTHOR

Louise Jeter Walker gave a lifetime in helping people understand Christian truths. She earned both BA and MA degrees in Christian education and was an ordained minister of the Assemblies of God (USA). Her books and materials reflect the experience of over sixty-two years of missionary service in Peru, Cuba, Central America, the West Indies, and Belgium.

God bless you as you begin to study *Your New Life*. May your heart be opened to the truths in God's Word.

Lessons
1. You Have Begun a New Life
2. You Are Learning to Walk
3. Your Father Is Speaking to You
4. Do You Want to Grow?
5. New Life, New Activities

LESSON 1
You Have Begun a New Life

What happens when a caterpillar becomes a butterfly? How does a seed become a great tree? Natural life is at work in each one, and it produces an amazing change. Now that you are a Christian, spiritual life is at work in you. The change will be much greater than what happens to a caterpillar or a seed. God is beginning to make you like Jesus Christ, His Son!

Like the butterfly, you will now enjoy new freedom to experience God's wonderful plan for your life. Like the tree, you will grow strong and fruitful. All this will happen because you have been born into God's family. You are now His child in a very special way.

In this first lesson, you will examine what the Bible says about the change that has happened to you. You will learn about your new privileges and responsibilities. You will discover the new family into which you have been born. You will find out about the new relationships that God wants you to build with your brothers and sisters in the Lord.

Lesson Outline

A. What Happened?

B. What Must You Do About It?

C. Your New Family

Lesson Goals

1. Discover what the Bible says about the change that has taken place in you.

2. State the steps you must take to grow strong as a Christian.

3. Describe the new relationships you have as a child of God.

A. WHAT HAPPENED?

Goal 1. Discover what the Bible says about the change that has taken place in you.

The moment you accepted Jesus Christ as your Savior, you began a new life. He is the giver of life—wonderful, rich, and joyful life that never ends. You gave your life with all of its sins and failures to Him, and He gave you His life of victory over sin. You have begun a life full of glorious privileges as a child of God.

Application

1 Your new life comes from
a) trying to be a Christian.
b) Jesus Christ, the giver of life.
c) joining a church.

2 You began a new life
a) the moment you accepted Jesus Christ as your Savior.
b) after you understood everything about being a Christian.
c) when you decided to become a better person.

You have this new life because Jesus lives in you. God's Word, the Bible, tells you about it.

> To them God has chosen to make known among the Gentiles the glorious riches of this mystery, which is Christ in you, the hope of glory. (Colossians 1:27)

NOTE: The reference at the end of the quotation you have just read (Colossians 1:27) tells you where you can find the quotation in your Bible. It lists the name of the book, the number of the chapter or chapters, and the number of the verse or verses.

Application

3 You learn about the life that comes from Jesus Christ living in you through
a) science and philosophy.
b) different religions.
c) God's Word, the Bible.

Christ living in you makes you a Christian. Some people think that a Christian life is a dull, prison-like existence. They think it means keeping a long list of rules. They could not be more mistaken! Your new life in Christ will be richer, fuller, and happier than you ever dreamed life could be. Jesus said, "The thief comes only to steal and kill and destroy; I have come that they may have life, and have it to the full" (John 10:10).

Application

4 Read the words of Jesus in John 10:10 until you can say them by memory.

5 Jesus Christ came to give you
a) punishment for your sins.
b) life in all its fullness.
c) rules and regulations.

In this life that Jesus gives, you will find new understanding, a new outlook, new goals, and a new purpose for living. The burden of guilt is gone; your sins are forgiven. A new love for God and for others fills your heart, bringing you peace and joy. You have a new appreciation for all that is good and beautiful and a new sense of God's presence, power, and goodness. New desires to please God and help others are beginning to change the direction of all your actions.

When a caterpillar becomes a butterfly, it can do things it never could before. It can fly above the places it once crawled. You have experienced an even greater change. The change the Holy Spirit has made in you affects everything. You have actually passed from death to life! You are no longer a guilty sinner. You have received God's pardon and are now His child. You can now have a life of true freedom and joy.

Application

6 In your own words, describe one way your life has changed since you asked Jesus Christ to be your Savior.

....
....

7 When you were born into God's family, you began a life of
a) escape from all problems.
b) freedom to act any way you please.
c) love for God and others.

B. What Must You Do About It?

Goal 2. State the steps you must take to grow strong as a Christian.

As a newborn baby in God's family, you will enjoy His loving care. You must also accept the provisions that He made to keep you healthy and strong. He has given you a new nature, and now you must do your part to develop it.

This book will help you develop your new nature. As you study these lessons, you will learn about your new privileges and responsibilities as a child of God. Enjoy them to the fullest during your life on earth. Then, someday Jesus will take you to live with Him in His heavenly home, a home that will be a thousand times more wonderful than anything in this world.

The main thing you must do is to maintain a relationship with Christ and grow strong in the life He gives. Jesus said, "Remain in me, and I will remain in you . . . apart from me you can do nothing" (John 15:4–5). Paul encourages,

> So then, just as you received Christ Jesus as Lord, continue to live in him, rooted and built up in him, strengthened in the faith as you were taught, and overflowing with thankfulness. (Colossians 2:6–7)

Application

8 The purpose of this course is to help you
a) discuss religion.
b) learn rules a Christian must follow.
c) enjoy all your privileges as a child of God.

9 You develop your new nature as a Christian by
a) maintaining a relationship with Christ.
b) trying hard to be like Jesus.
c) acting like other Christians.

C. Your New Family

Goal 3. Describe the new relationships you have as a child of God.

God Is Your Father

The Almighty God, who created the universe, is now your loving Father. Do not think of Him as being stern and far away. He is at your side right now, eager to help you in all your problems.

Now that you are a child of God, your Father wants you to talk with Him frankly and confidently, just as a child does to a kind and understanding father. Talk things over with Him in prayer every day, at any time of the day or night. Tell Him all your problems. Thank Him for His blessings. He is interested in you and everything that affects you. You do not have to use beautiful words or memorized prayers; just tell Him whatever is in your heart.

Application

10 In your new life, God is with you as a
a) far-off being.
b) loving Father.
c) demanding task master.

11 Circle the letter before each phrase that gives an example or description of how you can pray now that you have new life in Christ.
a) Thoughts from your heart
b) Memorized, carefully chosen words
c) By going as a child to your heavenly Father
d) Any time of day or night
e) Knowing He loves you
f) Only when you are in a church building

Jesus Christ Is Your Older Brother

Jesus Christ is your older brother in the family of God. He loves you so much that He died to save you. Now He wants to help you live a joyful life of victory over sin. Because He became a man and lived on earth, He understands the kind of problems you have. Thank Him now for saving you and for the help that He will give you each day.

Application

12 Complete the following sentence in your own words.

Jesus Christ is my older brother who understands me because He..

....

The Holy Spirit Is Your Helper

The Holy Spirit is the one who performed in you the mysterious miracle of new birth. He changed your sinful nature and made you a child of God.

You will still have to fight against the old nature at times, but the Holy Spirit has come to live in your heart and help you. As you cooperate with Him in faith and obedience, He will teach you what to do and give you strength to do it.

Application

13 The miracle of new life in you has been produced by the
a) Holy Spirit.
b) evangelist.
c) pastor.

14 The purpose of the Holy Spirit is to
a) punish you each time you make a mistake.
b) force you to do what God wants you to do.
c) live in you and help you do what is right.

Other Christians Are Your Brothers and Sisters

Every Christian has been born again and is a child of God. Since God is our Father, we are all brothers and sisters in Christ.

The older Christians all welcome you, their new brother or sister, into the family of God. They want to do everything they can to help you grow spiritually and become a strong, healthy Christian.

When you are facing a problem, talk it over with the pastor and with older believers in the church. They will pray with you about it and do whatever they can to help you.

Application

15 In your new life, other Christians are your brothers and sisters because they
a) attend services.
b) believe that religion is a good thing.
c) have the same heavenly Father that you do.

16 Write the number of the person or persons in your new family (right) before each phrase that describes the special relationship you have with Him or them (left).

....**a)** Lives in you to help you do God's will

....**b)** Can share your problems and pray with you

....**c)** Is your older brother who understands you

....**d)** Loves you and is your Father

....**e)** Died to save you

1) God
2) Jesus Christ
3) The Holy Spirit
4) Other Christians

Answers to Application Questions

The answers to your application study questions are not given in the usual order so that you will not see your next answer ahead of time. Look for the number you need, and try not to look ahead.

10 b) loving Father.

1 b) Jesus Christ, the giver of life.

11 a) Thoughts from your heart
 c) By going as a child to your heavenly Father
 d) Any time of day or night
 e) Knowing that He loves you

2 a) the moment you accepted Jesus Christ as your Savior.

12 Your answer should be something like this: . . . lived on earth as a man and faced the same kinds of problems I face.

3 c) God's Word, the Bible.

13 a) Holy Spirit.

5 b) life in all its fullness.

14 c) live in you and help you do what is right.

7 c) love for God and others.

15 c) have the same heavenly Father that you do.

8 c) enjoy all your privileges as a child of God.

16 a) 3) The Holy Spirit
 b) 4) Other Christians
 c) 2) Jesus Christ
 d) 1) God
 e) 2) Jesus Christ

9 a) maintaining a relationship with Christ.

You Have Begun a New Life

LESSON 2
You Are Learning to Walk

Have you ever watched a child who is learning to walk? Barely able to stand, the little one wobbles and totters around the room, holding onto whatever can be reached. But what excitement! What a look—as if the whole world had been conquered! Sometimes moving, sometimes standing, sometimes falling—but always getting up again and going on—the child learns to walk. The desire to succeed is strong. All the time the parents are close by, reaching out to help and encourage every step.

You are like that child in some ways. You have a new life from God. But learning how to live it is like learning how to walk. You need to be strong in your desire to succeed. Your heavenly Father is close by, ready to help. But you must try. You must put your hand in His hand and keep trying. If you do, every day you will improve. Your steps will become more firm and sure. You will stumble less often. Your ability will grow, and you will fulfill God's wonderful plan for your life.

Lesson Outline

A. Put Your Hand in God's Hand

B. Face Problems with God's Help

C. Do What God Asks You to Do

Lesson Goals

1. Describe what it means to walk with Christ.

2. Discover how to overcome discouragement, opposition, and doubt.

3. Take steps to make sure of your salvation.

A. PUT YOUR HAND IN GOD'S HAND

Goal 1. Describe what it means to walk with Christ.

How happy parents are when their baby takes his or her first steps. How happy your heavenly Father is when you, His child, begin to walk with Him in this Christian life. Do not be afraid you will fall; just put your hand in your Father's and He will help you. Each day, as you awake, ask Him to help you in everything you do that day.

Application

1 The way to learn how to walk in your new life is to
a) place confidence in yourself and your abilities.
b) put your hand in God's and trust Him to help you.
c) wait until you know everything you should do.

B. Face Problems with God's Help

Goal 2. Discover how to overcome discouragement, opposition, and doubt.

Has Satan Tried to Make You Fall?

Satan, the devil, is an enemy of God and of every Christian. He tries to trip you up and make you fall. He may use persecution, ridicule, discouragement, or temptation. He will try to make you doubt you are saved. Satan always fights against Christians and tries to take them away from God. He especially seeks to confuse new Christians with doubts and difficulties. He does not want you to learn to walk with God.

So do not be surprised if you get a few bumps while you are learning to walk. Children may run into a chair and hurt themselves, or lose their balance and fall, but this is no reason for them to refuse to try to walk again.

Application

2 Circle the letter before each true statement.
a) Satan often tries to make new Christians doubt their salvation.
b) Discouragement is a sign that God is angry with you.
c) After you become a Christian, you will have no more problems.
d) As a new Christian, you can expect that Satan will fight against you.

Remember that your heavenly Father is much stronger than the devil, and He will hold your hand. John 10:28 says of Jesus, "I give them eternal life, and they shall never perish; no one can snatch them out of my hand."

Application

3 Memorize the words of Jesus in John 10:28.

Are You Suffering for Christ's Sake?

Do not be surprised or angry if your family or some of your friends make fun of you for accepting Christ. They may even persecute you. It is an honor and privilege to suffer for the One who died on the cross for us. We *carry our crosses* and follow Him, letting Him know that we appreciate what He suffered for our sakes.

The Lord promises to reward those who suffer for His sake. Luke 9:23 records: "He said to them all: 'If anyone would come after me, he must deny himself and take up his cross daily and follow me.'"

Blessed are those who are persecuted because of righteousness, for theirs is the kingdom of heaven. Blessed are you when people insult you, persecute you and falsely say all kinds of evil against you because of me. Rejoice and be glad, because great is your reward in heaven, for in the same way they persecuted the prophets who were before you. (Matthew 5:10–12)

Application

4 Jesus said that when you suffer because you are His follower, you should be
- **a)** sad and discouraged.
- **b)** angry and ready to fight back.
- **c)** happy because He will reward you.

Are You Discouraged or Bothered with Doubts?

Do not be discouraged if you have a hard time doing what is right. When new Christians make a mistake, the devil tries to discourage them by making them think, "Now look at what I've done. I must not be a child of God, or I would act differently."

Some new Christians become confused and give way to doubt. They think, "I can't live a Christian life; it's too hard for me. I might as well go back to my old life. Besides, I don't see the great change in myself that the Christians talk about. I don't feel any joy of salvation. I guess I am not a Christian after all."

Have you struggled with some of these doubts? Remember that they come from your enemy who is trying to discourage you and make you fall. Some people feel more joy than others when they get saved, so do not worry about how you feel. The more you learn about what God did when He made you His child, the more joy you will have. As you thank Him for His blessings, your joy will grow. *Remember that your salvation does not depend on what you feel; it depends on the faithfulness of God to you and your faith and trust in God.*

If you have stumbled and fallen, it does not mean that you cannot learn to walk or that you are not God's child. Ask His forgiveness for your failures, and then get up and try again.

As to the change in yourself, your desire to please God and the fact that you worry over your failures are proofs of a new nature. So do not be discouraged. Remember that some children have more trouble than others in learning to walk.

Application

5 Circle the letter before the true statement.
a) Real Christians always feel happy.
b) All Christians feel the same amount of joy when God saves them.
c) Thanking God for His blessings will cause your joy to grow.

6 Your salvation depends on the
a) feelings you have.
b) faithfulness of God toward you and your trust in Him.
c) number of good things you have done.

Your Father Loves You

Do you suppose that loving parents would scold their baby for falling down, or go off and leave the child when he or she is hurt? Not at all! They would pick up the baby, offer comfort, and then encourage the child to keep on trying until he or she learns to walk well. Do you think God will do any less for His child who is beginning to walk? No! Look to Him now in prayer and tell Him, "Thank you, Father, for holding my hand and teaching me how to walk. I am weak, but I know you will help me do what I ought to do."

You should know that God guides you in your Christian life by His Holy Spirit and by His Word, the Holy Bible. Read the Bible and pray every day. This will help you get rid of your doubts and walk without stumbling.

Application

7 If you have done something you should not have done, you can expect your heavenly Father to
a) forgive you and help you to do better.
b) be angry and disown you as His child.
c) leave you alone in your guilt.

8 What should you do each day so that God can guide you?

....
....

C. Do What God Asks You to Do

Goal 3. Take steps to make sure of your salvation.

Maybe you are wondering if you have done everything God expects you to do to be saved. Christ tells us clearly what a person has to do to be saved, so let us see now if you have done your part. God asks you to do two things to be saved: repent of your sins and believe the gospel.

Repent

Mark records the words of Jesus: "'The time has come,' he said. 'The kingdom of God is near. Repent and believe the good news!'" (Mark 1:15). To repent means to be sorry for your sins and turn away from them.

Are you sorry for having disobeyed God? Are you determined to get rid of sin in your life, or is there some sin that you want to hold on to? Are you willing to give up your own way and, from now on, do only what pleases God?

Application

9 Circle the letter before the two phrases that state what God asks you to do to be saved.
a) Do penance.
b) Join the church.
c) Believe the gospel.
d) Fast for several days.
e) Repent of your sins.
f) Do good deeds.
g) Give money to the church.

10 Memorize the words of Jesus in Mark 1:15.

11 To repent means to
a) be sorry for your sins and turn away from them.
b) confess all your sins to a priest.
c) tell other people that you want to change.

Has someone treated you so badly that you do not want to forgive him or her? Hatred and resentment keep many people from a relationship with God. God is love, and He cannot live in a heart full of hate and prejudice. If you have something against someone, forgive that person now, and ask God to help you love those who have treated you so badly. Jesus said, "If you do not forgive men their sins, your Father will not forgive your sins" (Matthew 6:15).

If you still doubt that you have repented sincerely, you can settle this at once. Turn away from all sin and give up your way of doing things so God can have His way in your life from now on.

Application

12 If someone has done something wrong to you, you should
a) tell everyone how bad he or she is.
b) forgive that person right now.
c) plan how you can punish him or her.

Believe the Gospel of Jesus Christ

The word *gospel* means "good news." It refers to the good news about salvation in Jesus Christ. The following gospel teachings are found in the Bible. Write *yes* after those you believe.

- God loved you so much that He sent His Son Jesus to take the punishment for your sins. ....

- Jesus died for your sins and will free you from them when you accept Him as Savior and Lord. ....

- Jesus rose from the dead and went back to heaven. He prays for you and is preparing a home for you. ....

- When you accept Jesus as your Savior, you become a child of God and have a new life in Him. ....

- Jesus will come back for His own and take them back with Him to their eternal home in heaven. ....

- Do you believe all this about Jesus Christ? ....

- Have you accepted Jesus as your personal Savior? ....

Then trust in Him and believe His promises. Luke records this promise: "Believe in the Lord Jesus, and you will be saved—

you and your household" (Acts 16:31). John also encourages us, "God has given us eternal life, and this life is in his Son. He who has the Son has life; he who does not have the Son of God does not have life" (1 John 5:11–12).

Application

13 Why do you think the gospel of Jesus Christ is called the "good news"?

....
....

14 Memorize 1 John 5:11–12.

Believing in Jesus means you trust in Him. He understands and loves you. He prays to the Father for you. Jesus is the one that God has chosen to do this. Paul wrote, "For there is one God and one mediator between God and men, the man Christ Jesus" (1 Timothy 2:5). Peter also taught that "Salvation is found in no one else, for there is no other name under heaven given to men by which we must be saved" (Acts 4:12).

Jesus said, "I am the way and the truth and the life. No one comes to the Father except through me" (John 14:6). There is no other road or way to God. You cannot walk on two roads at the same time. You will have to leave any other way that claims to lead you to God in order to follow Jesus, the only true way. You will have to place all of your faith in Him.

If you have really repented, believing God's promises and trusting in Christ as your only Savior, you are saved.

Application

15 Following are some facts about Jesus Christ. Which one makes Him the only way to God?
a) He is a good and wise teacher.
b) He is unselfish and loving.
c) He is humble, yet strong.
d) He is the perfect Son of God, who died for our sins.

Do you want to make sure Jesus is your Savior? Do you want to rededicate your life to God and ensure that you are walking with Him? Tell Him so in the words of this prayer:

Prayer

Thank You, God, for Your love for me and for sending Your only Son, Jesus Christ, to die in my place. I accept Him as my Savior and Master. Thank You for forgiving my sins and accepting me as Your child. Help me to be good and obedient and to please You in all things. I give myself to You. Help me to walk with You all the rest of my life. Amen.

Answers to Application Questions

8 Read the Bible and pray.

1 b) put your hand in God's and trust Him to help you.

9 c) Believe the gospel.
e) Repent of your sins.

2 Statements **a)** and **d)** are true.

11 a) be sorry for your sins and turn away from them.

4 c) happy because He will reward you.

12 b) forgive that person right now.

5 Statement **c)** is true.

13 Your answer. The gospel is "good news" because it tells us that we do not have to work for our salvation. Jesus Christ gives it to us as a free gift when we repent of our sins and believe in Him.

6 b) faithfulness of God toward you and your trust in Him.

15 d) Perfect Son of God who died for our sins

7 a) forgive you and help you to do better.

LESSON 3
Your Father Is Speaking to You

How does a sheep know when to graze on the hillside and when to go into the fold? How does it avoid following a stranger? A sheep is led and protected by listening to the voice of its shepherd. Because the shepherd has cared for the sheep since it was a lamb, the sheep knows the shepherd's voice. It follows no one else.

In some ways, your relationship to God is like that of a sheep to its shepherd. God wants to lead you and care for you. He speaks to you every day to guide and protect you from danger. As you listen to His voice, you will be able to recognize it more. You will know the right things to do, even when others try to confuse you.

This lesson will help you understand how God speaks to you. Sometimes He will speak to you directly. At other times He will use His Word, the Bible. At still other times, He will use another Christian.

As you study this lesson, you will discover how to recognize your Father's voice no matter what method He chooses.

Lesson Outline

A. God Wants to Talk to You

B. God Speaks in Many Ways

C. God Has a Book for You

D. How to Hear God's Voice

Lesson Goals

1. Give reasons why you can expect God to talk to you.

2. State several ways God speaks to you.

3. Describe the Book God has for you.

4. Know how to hear God's voice every day.

A. GOD WANTS TO TALK TO YOU

Goal 1. Give reasons why you can expect God to talk to you.

What father does not enjoy talking with his children even when they are babies and can only answer with a smile? Your heavenly Father also likes to talk with His children, showing His love for them, teaching them, and helping them with their problems. Would you like to hear His voice?

Application

1 You can expect God to talk to you because He
a) loves you as your heavenly Father.
b) made everything that exists.
c) is able to do anything He decides to do.

B. God Speaks in Many Ways

Goal 2. State several ways God speaks to you.

Hebrews 1:1–2 says, "In the past God spoke to our forefathers through the prophets at many times and in various ways, but in these last days he has spoken to us by his Son, whom he appointed heir of all things, and through whom he made the universe." Here are some of the ways God speaks to you.

Directly to Your Heart

The Holy Spirit makes the presence of Jesus known to you. He may speak through your conscience, making you feel what you ought to do or warning you not to do something. He may make a spiritual truth clear to you. Or you may feel a deep impression that God wants you to do something. When you pray, ask God to speak to you and expect to hear His voice in your heart.

Application

2   How does God speak directly to your heart? Circle the two correct statements.

a) You always hear a distinct voice just like you would if a person were speaking to you.
b) You may be impressed to do something.
c) God's voice must be through a dream or a vision.
d) A spiritual truth may suddenly become real or clear to you.

Through His Blessings

Many Christians say that the whole world looks different to them since they have been born again. You too may have a new appreciation of God's blessings as you look around. You can feel His presence in the wonders of nature. He speaks to you through music and art. You feel Him near in the warm friendship of other Christians. A thousand blessings all around you tell you of the goodness of God. He speaks in the answers to your prayers. Through faith, you hear Him say, "I love you and want to bless you."

Application

3   Name a blessing in which you can see that God loves you.

....

....

Through Other Christians

Sometimes the older children in a family say to the younger, "No, no! Mommy doesn't like that!" Or, "Look, this is what Daddy wants."

God, too, speaks to His children through older brothers and sisters in the Lord. He wants us to meet often with other Christians so He can use them to encourage, guide, and help us. Paul encourages us to "be filled with the Spirit . . . Submit to one another out of reverence for Christ" (Ephesians 5:18, 21).

Application

4   Have other Christians ever helped you understand what God wanted you to do?

....

....

....

5   Has anyone encouraged you to be a better Christian? ......
    Who? ....

6   Thank God now for the way He speaks to you through other Christians. Ask Him to speak to you to help others find salvation or encourage others to follow the Lord.

Through Spiritual Gifts and Ministries

The Holy Spirit has put in the church many different spiritual gifts. He speaks to us through them. He gives God's message for the church to pastors, teachers, evangelists, and writers. He wants to use every Christian to tell about God. It is important for you to attend church services as often as you can. Every time you go, listen for what your heavenly Father wants to tell you. Jesus taught, "Where two or three come together in my name, there am I with them" (Matthew 18:20).

Application

7 From the following list, choose three ways God speaks to people.
a) The preaching of evangelists
b) Spiritual mediums
c) Witchcraft
d) Christian pastors
e) Books by Christian writers

8 When you are in church, do you expect God to speak to you? ....

9 Has God spoken to you through this book? ....
Ask Him to speak to you in every lesson.

Through Songs

God will often speak to you through the words of a gospel song or chorus. You will be surprised to see how often He will bring to your mind the words of some song just when you need its message. Thus, Paul urged the believers in Ephesus to "speak to one another with psalms, hymns and spiritual songs. Sing and make music in your heart to the Lord" (Ephesians 5:19).

Application

10 Ask the Lord to help you quickly learn the songs and hymns sung at your church. Sing them at home as much as you can.

11 Make a habit of thinking about what you are singing. Is there a song with a certain truth you want to become part of your life? Write that truth in the following space, and ask God to help you apply it to your life.

....
....

Through the Bible

God speaks to you through His book, the Holy Bible. This is the surest way of knowing His message. The pastor may not always know what God's will is for you. Your brothers and sisters in Christ might give you wrong advice. Dreams and visions are not always from God. They can come from what you have been thinking about or from your subconscious. You may feel God wants you to do something when it is your own desire urging you to do it. So how can you know God's voice?

You have God's message written for you in the Bible. You must test everything else by what God tells you in the Bible. That is why it is so important to study God's Word as you are doing now. Through these basic studies you will understand the Bible better. You will also learn how to put its teachings into practice in your life.

> Open my eyes that I may see wonderful things in your law. (Psalm 119:18)

> Your word, O LORD, is eternal; it stands firm in the heavens. (Psalm 119:89)

> Your word is a lamp to my feet and a light for my path. (Psalm 119:105)

The unfolding of your words gives light; it gives understanding to the simple. (Psalm 119:130)

All your words are true; all your righteous laws are eternal. (Psalm 119:160)

Application

12 What is the surest way to know God's message for you?
a) Study what God says in the Bible.
b) Listen to the advice of your friends.
c) Follow your feelings about what you should do.

C. GOD HAS A BOOK FOR YOU

Goal 3. Describe the Book God has for you.

How God's Book Was Written

The Bible is made up of sixty-six different books. Over a period of around sixteen hundred years, about forty different men wrote these books. These were men God chose, and He sent His Holy Spirit to help them know what to write. As a result, we have God's message to us. Together, the sixty-six books are called the Holy Scriptures. All agree perfectly with each other. They develop the same theme in such unity that we know they have come from one single Author—God.

Application

13 Which statements below are true?
a) Although the Bible has sixty-six different books, it has only one theme.
b) The Holy Spirit guided each man who wrote a book of the Bible so he would know what to write.
c) All sixty-six books of the Bible were written at the same time.

Godly people recognized the special quality of the sixty-six books God had inspired. About two hundred years after Jesus was born, the sixty-six books were compiled into one book, the Holy Bible. *Holy Bible* means the books of God. The first thirty-nine books were written before the birth of our Lord Jesus. They are called the Old Testament. The second part of the Bible is called the New Testament. In it are the twenty-seven books written after Jesus came and made a new covenant between God and humankind. They give us the terms of this covenant.

Most of the Old Testament was first written in Hebrew, and the New Testament in Greek. A small part of the Old Testament was written in Aramaic. God has given us His book for all humankind and wants everybody to read it. He has helped His children translate it into many languages. Now there are parts of the Bible in more than three thousand languages.

Application

14 Match the part of the Bible (right) to each phrase that describes it (left).

....**a)** Describes the new covenant   1) Old Testament

....**b)** Mostly written in Hebrew   2) New Testament

....**c)** twenty-seven books

....**d)** thirty-nine books

....**e)** Written in Greek

....**f)** Written before Jesus was born

In some languages there are several different translations, or versions, of the Bible. A Christian pastor or teacher may be able to help you choose the best translation in your language. Scripture quotations in this book (*Your New Life*) are taken from the *New International Version* of the Bible.

Application

15 The Bible is a book for
a) only the well educated who can read Hebrew, Aramaic, and Greek.
b) everyone.
c) ministers or pastors and no one else.

Bible References

Each book of the Bible is divided into numbered chapters. The chapters are divided into small paragraphs called verses. The verses are numbered so we can tell exactly where to find what we are looking for in the Bible. If you want to make a note of where a certain passage is found in the Bible, you write first the name of the book, then the number of the chapter followed by a colon (:), and the number of the verse. For example, "John 3:16" refers to the book of John, chapter 3, verse 16. This is a Scripture reference.

To refer to two or more verses that are not consecutive, separate them by commas. "John 3:16, 18, 20" means John, chapter 3, verses 16, 18, and 20.

An en dash between two numbers means that all the verses in between are included. "John 3:16–22" means John, chapter 3, verses 16 through 22.

An en dash is also used between two consecutive verses. "John 3:16–17" means John, chapter 3, verses 16 and 17.

When referring to verses in different chapters, use a semicolon (;) to separate the references. "John 3:16; 6:24" means John, chapter 3, verse 16; and John, chapter 6, verse 24.

Application

16 The Scripture reference for the book of Matthew, chapter 6, verses 31, 32 and 33 should be written as
a) Matthew 31–32, and 33.
b) Matthew 6:31, 32, and 33.
c) Matthew 6:31–33

17 The reference "Luke 13:18–19; 20:25–26" means
a) chapter 13 of Luke, verses 18, 19, 20, 25, and 26.
b) Luke, chapter 13, verses 18 and 19; and Luke, chapter 20, verses 25 and 26.
c) Luke chapters 13,18,19, 20, 25, and 26.

D. How to Hear God's Voice

Goal 4. Know how to hear God's voice every day.

Before listening to a certain station on the radio, you must set your dial to tune it in. How can you set the dial of your spirit to tune in God's voice? Here are a few ways to do it.

- Read the Bible every day.

- Keep thinking about what you have read in the Bible. Meditate on God's Word.

- Make a habit of rereading and memorizing Bible verses you especially like.

> All Scripture is God-breathed and is useful
> for teaching, rebuking, correcting and training
> in righteousness, so that the man of God may
> be thoroughly equipped for every good work.
> (2 Timothy 3:16–17)

If you are just now starting to read the Bible, begin with the book of Mark in the New Testament. God will speak to you very clearly through Jesus' life and teachings, and it will help you understand the Old Testament.

> In the past God spoke to our forefathers through the prophets at many times and in various ways, but in these last days he has spoken to us by his Son, whom he appointed heir of all things, and through whom he made the universe. (Hebrews 1:1–2)

- Go to church regularly, expecting to hear from God.
- Pray every day. Ask God to speak to you. When you pray, you may want to close your eyes to "tune out" thoughts about the things around you. Do not use all the time talking to God. Wait quietly for Him to speak to your heart.
- Sing gospel songs and think about their words.
- Practice looking for God's goodness, power, and love all around you.
- Read Christian literature and listen to gospel broadcasts when you can.
- Talk with other Christians about God and His Word.
- Do what God tells you to do. Remember that to have Him lead you, you must be willing to follow.
- Faithfully do your lessons in this book and other Bible studies, and ask God to speak to you through them.

Application

18 Go back over the list of things you can do to hear God's voice. Put a check mark beside each one that you are already doing. Pray about each one that you are not doing yet or that you are not doing regularly. Underline each one that you plan to start doing.

Answers to Application Questions

13 Statements **a)** and **b)** are true.

1 **a)** loves you as your heavenly Father.

14 **a)** 2) New Testament
   b) 1) Old Testament
   c) 2) New Testament
   d) 1) Old Testament
   e) 2) New Testament
   f) 1) Old Testament

2 Statements **b)** and **d)** are correct.

15 **b)** everyone.

7 **a)** The preaching of evangelists
   d) Christian pastors
   e) Books by Christian writers

16 **c)** Matthew 6:31–33.

12 **a)** Study what God says in the Bible.

17 **b)** Luke, chapter 13, verses 18 and 19; and Luke, chapter 20, verses 25 and 26.

LESSON 4: Do You Want to Grow?

You have been born into God's family. Now you need to grow. How can you do this? In some ways spiritual growth is like physical growth. To grow physically, you must eat the right foods, get the proper amount of rest, avoid harm and danger, and get enough exercise.

To grow spiritually, you must do similar things. Spiritual growth does not just happen. God has planned for you to take an active part in the changes He wants to make in your life. You must learn to feed your soul on God's Word, rest in His promises, avoid things that will destroy your spiritual health, and choose to do what He says will make you strong. If you follow these steps each day, you will discover the "abundant life" God has promised to His children.

This lesson explains more about these four important principles of spiritual growth. As you study the principles, you will see how you can put them into practice in your own life. Wonderful results will follow. Harmful actions in your life will be replaced by good ones, and you will grow daily into the mature person God wants you to become.

Lesson Outline

A. Feed Your Soul Every Day

B. Rest in the Lord

C. Keep Spiritually Healthy

D. Exercise Your Spiritual Muscles

Lesson Goals

1. Identify ways to grow spiritually.

2. Use biblical tools to overcome discouragement and worry.

3. Show the importance of maintaining your spiritual health.

4. Point out ways to serve God better.

A. FEED YOUR SOUL EVERY DAY

Goal 1. Identify ways to grow spiritually.

Talking with God feeds your soul. God speaks to you through His Word, and you speak to Him in prayer. Jesus said, "It is written: 'Man does not live on bread alone, but on every word that comes from the mouth of God'" (Matthew 4:4). Peter also teaches, "Like newborn babies, crave pure spiritual milk, so that by it you may grow up in your salvation" (1 Peter 2:2). The Word of God, the Bible, is the spiritual milk you must drink often.

Does the Bible seem hard to understand? Before you start reading it each day, ask the Lord to make it clear to you. Ask other Christians or your pastor any questions you may have about it.

Take advantage of every opportunity to receive Bible teaching in Sunday school, other church services, and special courses like this one. You can also feed your soul with gospel literature.

Do you want to grow rapidly in the Lord? Eat well. You should read at least one chapter a day from the New Testament.

This part of the Bible tells about our Lord Jesus Christ and teaches us how we ought to live. It is good to learn some of the verses you especially like. In this way you develop an appetite for the Word of God.

> Oh, how I love your law! I meditate on it all day long. (Psalm 119:97)
>
> How sweet are your words to my taste, sweeter than honey to my mouth! (Psalm 119:103)

Application

1 Following are listed several activities. Choose those that will help you grow spiritually.
a) Reading Christian literature
b) Arguing with others about religion
c) Doing penance and religious rituals
d) Studying the Bible and praying to God

2 Will you sign this promise?
Lord, with Your help I will try to read some of Your Word every day of my life. When I cannot read it, I will quote portions of it from memory or ask someone to read it to me. I will feed my soul on Your Word.

Signed ....

Date ....

B. Rest in the Lord

Goal 2. Use biblical tools to overcome discouragement and worry.

Do you feel too weak to do what the Lord wants you to do? You cannot go to heaven by your own efforts to be good or because of any good works you have done. You are on your way there because you are a child of God. He will take care of you. Let your faith rest in His promises.

Have your first steps with the Lord been unsteady? Have you stumbled and fallen and felt it is no use trying? Take courage. Your Father, who gave you this new life, is holding your hand and will lift you up again. Rest in His presence. Commit yourself each day to God in prayer, confessing your own weakness and asking Him to give you the strength to overcome every temptation. "But those who hope in the Lord will renew their strength. They will soar on wings like eagles; they will run and not grow weary, they will walk and not be faint" (Isaiah 40:31).

Do life's problems bother you? Are you afraid? Do you feel discouraged because you are overworked? Rest in the Lord so that worry, discouragement, and fear will not slow or stop your spiritual growth.

Do you know how to get this rest? Have faith. Believe what God has promised and look to Him instead of at your problems. Read Jesus' words:

> Come to me, all you who are weary
> and burdened, and I will give you rest.
> (Matthew 11:28)

> So do not worry, saying, "What shall we eat?" or "What shall we drink?" or "What shall we wear?" For the pagans run after all these things, and your heavenly Father knows that you need them. But seek first his kingdom and his righteousness, and all these things will be given to you as well. (Matthew 6:31–33)

Taking time for Bible reading and prayer every day will help you reach this place of rest in God. As you pray, put every problem in the Lord's hands and leave it there, believing He will do what is best.

Application

3 Memorize Isaiah 40:31. This verse says that those who find their strength renewed are those who

. . . .

4 Read carefully Matthew 11:28 and Matthew 6:31–33.

5 Is there something you are worrying about right now? Ask God to help you give this worry to Him so you can be free to serve Him and His kingdom instead.

C. Keep Spiritually Healthy

Goal 3. Show the importance of maintaining your spiritual health.

Avoid Disease: Stay Clean

Just like a mother tries to keep her children clean and protects them from things that would make them sick, the Lord wants to keep you away from things that would make your soul sick. When He saved you, He washed away your sins and gave you a clean heart. It is very important to keep it that way if you want to be spiritually healthy.

Let the Lord walk with you and be your guide. Stay out of the filth of indecent amusements and immoral living. Do not go where the Lord would not go. Keep clean in your thoughts, words, and actions.

Application

6 God wants you to avoid indecent amusements and immoral practices because He does not want you to
a) become spiritually weak and sick.
b) relax and enjoy life.
c) spend time with unbelievers.

Jesus taught, "Blessed are the pure in heart, for they will see God" (Matthew 5:8). What you think about is important! If you let your mind dwell on unclean thoughts, they will infect your soul, weaken your will, and cause you to fall into sin.

Do You Want to Grow?

You can ask God to stop you from actually doing things that are against His will. However, your responsibility does not end there. If you want to please Him, you must also stop thinking about doing such things. Ask God to help you shut out bad thoughts. Do not read books, look at pictures, or listen to stories that are indecent and immoral.

How can you control your thoughts? You must take positive steps to keep them pure. Here is what the Bible says:

> Finally, brothers, whatever is true, whatever is noble, whatever is right, whatever is pure, whatever is lovely, whatever is admirable—if anything is excellent or praiseworthy—think about such things. (Philippians 4:8)

Make this verse your daily prayer:

> May the words of my mouth and the meditation of my heart be pleasing in your sight, O Lord, my Rock and my Redeemer. (Psalm 19:14)

Application

7 Circle the letter before each true statement.

a) Thoughts can be controlled with God's help.
b) Bad thoughts are impossible to control.
c) The Bible tells us to fill our minds with good thoughts.
d) A person who is a Christian never thinks bad thoughts.
e) The only step you must take to control your thoughts is to ask God to take bad thoughts away.

8 Perhaps you struggle with bad thoughts. Review the steps you need to take. Underline each one you will begin doing now.

I will ask for God's help.

I will meditate on God's Word, the Bible.

I will fill my mind with good things.

I will avoid books, magazines, pictures, TV programs, movies, and internet sites that are evil and immoral.

It is easier to give yourself completely to the Lord than it is to serve Him halfheartedly. Do not play with sin. Get rid of anything in your life that would make you spiritually sick.

> But if we walk in the light, as he is in the light, we have fellowship with one another, and the blood of Jesus, his Son, purifies us from all sin . . . If we confess our sins, he is faithful and just and will forgive us our sins and purify us from all unrighteousness. (1 John 1:7, 9)

The blood of Jesus washes us clean from our sinful acts and sinful thoughts.

Avoid Disease: Do Not Take Poison

Certain attitudes or feelings are poisonous to both soul and body. Anger, worry, envy, hatred, suspicion, fear, resentment, and impatience can cause indigestion, ulcers, heart trouble, and other diseases. They choke our spiritual life too and cause all kinds of trouble such as pride, selfishness, unbelief, and stubbornness. They take away a Christian's joy and leave the soul weak, sickly, and unhappy. Each day ask God to keep you from taking any of this poison.

If you ever feel weak and sick spiritually, remember that Jesus is the Great Physician. Go to Him sincerely in prayer, and He will give you spiritual, mental, and physical health.

Application

9 Listed below are some poisons you must keep out of your mind. Underline those that are a problem for you, and ask God to help you overcome them.

Anger	Hatred	Resentment
Worry	Suspicion	Impatience
Envy	Fear	

D. Exercise Your Spiritual Muscles

Goal 4. Point out ways to serve God better.

The body is strengthened by exercise, while the soul is strengthened by working for God. From the first day of your new life, there are several things you can do to show your gratitude to the Lord for His salvation.

Some of these spiritual exercises are telling others about Jesus, praying for them, and inviting them to church. Taking part in church and fighting against sin will help you grow spiritually. As you grow spiritually and learn more of His Word, the Lord will give you more opportunities and responsibilities in His work.

Application

10 Describe something you can do this week to make your spiritual life stronger.

> Therefore, my dear brothers, stand firm. Let nothing move you. Always give yourselves fully to the work of the Lord, because you know that your labor in the Lord is not in vain. (1 Corinthians 15:58)

Answers to Application Questions

6 a) become spiritually weak and sick.

1 Activities **a)** and **d)** will help you grow spiritually.

7 Statements **a)** and **c)** are true.

3 hope in the Lord.

LESSON 5
New Life, New Activities

When we were children, we did the things children do. We played games and explored our surroundings. We liked to run, jump, and play. Our responsibilities were few, because our parents cared for us.

But life changed when we became adults. We began to take care of ourselves. We formed our own families and began to provide for them. What we did in our spare time also changed. As our interests and skills developed, so did our activities.

A similar change is taking place in your life right now. Your spiritual life is unfolding. As you "grow up" in Christ, new interests replace old ones. There are also new responsibilities—ones that can bring you new kinds of rewards and satisfactions. In this lesson, we will look at these special changes and activities. You will discover also that other people share your new interests!

Lesson Outline

A. New Interests

B. New Activities

C. New Testimony

D. New Partnership

Lesson Goals

1. Identify the new interests you have.
2. Join with others who have the same new interests you have.
3. Choose to tell others about your faith in Jesus Christ.
4. Identify ways you can partner with God.

A. New Interests

Goal 1. Identify the new interests you have.

How Do You Spend Your Time?

Of course you have to spend a certain number of hours each day working, eating, and sleeping; but how do you spend the rest of your time? What people do in their free time depends on what interests them and their families. Some work all the time, and others play. Some go to church and take part in its work; others do not. You probably do not have enough time to do everything that you would like to do, but somehow you manage to find time for the things that interest you most.

Application

1 What people do in their free time is usually determined by
a) how much time they have.
b) their main interests.
c) the opinions of others.

When Your Interests Change

You do not play the same games that you liked when you were a little child because you are busy doing something that interests you more now. When your interests change, so do your activities.

Your old friends may be surprised that you are no longer interested in "having a good time" with them in things that would harm your health or hurt your soul. They may not understand that you have entered a life of deeper enjoyment, full of worthwhile, satisfying activities.

Should you go back to the things you know cannot satisfy? Ask the man who is eating spoiled scraps from a garbage heap and then is invited to eat at a rich friend's table every day. Would he go back to the garbage dump?

Application

2 Describe a new interest you have since you accepted Jesus as your Savior.

....
....

3 Describe something you do now that you did not do before you accepted Jesus.

....
....

A Different Purpose

As a child of God, you have new interests. These will lead you into group activities and personal responsibilities. You will still do many of the things you used to do—work, eat, sleep, and take care of home duties—but your real life will center around your new interests.

Above all, when you love somebody, you want to be with and please that person. Now that you love God, you will want to spend time with Him and please Him in all you do.

Application

4 The different purpose you have as a child of God is to
a) try to make more money.
b) enjoy yourself and the good things of life.
c) spend time with your heavenly Father.

We are intensely interested in our Father's kingdom and what He is doing on earth. He is at work now, bringing men, women, and children to himself through the preaching of the good news about Jesus. He is building His church, and He has called us to work with Him. What a privilege!

Application

5 We have a part in what God is doing in the world today by
a) explaining the way of salvation to others.
b) ruling over those who are not Christians.
c) doing many religious rituals and ceremonies.

B. NEW ACTIVITIES

Goal 2. Join with others who have the same new interests you have.

Your new interests in God's kingdom will keep you busy and happy. Here are some activities that will give new purpose and meaning to your life.

Church Attendance

God's plan is for each Christian to become a member of a local church community. In keeping with this plan, Christians who live near each other meet together regularly to worship God, encourage each other, study the Bible, and share their faith with people who need to know about Jesus Christ. This is how they help each other do the work God has given them to do.

These meetings, or church services, may be held in someone's home or in a building dedicated to God for this purpose. You will want to attend these services as often as you can and take your friends with you to hear the gospel. You will enjoy the fellowship with your brothers and sisters in Christ and, most of all, the presence of the Lord as you meet with Him in these services.

As soon as possible, you will want to become a member of a church that serves God and preaches the gospel. Take part in its program, and enjoy its advantages and blessings. These lessons will help you become a good member.

Application

6 The paragraphs you have just read describe four activities Christians do when they meet together. In the following list, one of these activities is missing. Write it in the space provided.

- Listening to messages from the Bible
- Praising God and thanking Him
- Witnessing about their faith
- ....

What would happen if someday the pastor, or another Christian, should unintentionally offend you? When one child hurts another's feelings in a family, the children do not usually leave home over it. But when this happens in church, some Christians revolt and refuse to return to church. Instead, they choose to stay home under the guise of worshiping God there. Be careful! That is a favorite trick the devil uses to weaken a Christian and separate him or her from the Lord.

Remember that your Father expects His children to meet with Him in His house. The building may be humble, and you may not agree with the way everything is done, but you need to meet with your brothers and sisters in Christ to worship the Lord, study His Word together, and strengthen one another. Hebrews 10:24–25 advises, "Let us consider how we may spur one another on toward love and good deeds. Let us not give up meeting together, as some are in the habit of doing, but let us encourage one another—and all the more as you see the Day approaching."

Application

7 If the pastor says something that offends you, you should
a) quit going to church or find another church.
b) tell others he or she is not a good pastor.
c) forgive him or her and keep attending services.

8 One who believes it is not important to meet with other Christians should be reminded of the biblical instruction in

....

Bible Reading

We have already mentioned the importance of reading the Bible every day. Can you get the other members of your family to join with you daily for Bible reading and prayer? We call this a family altar, or family devotions. Having family devotions each day will be a real blessing to your home. The truth from God's Word that you share will guide and strengthen you for the day. When you meet, you can take time to pray together for the needs of each person in your family.

Application

9 Perhaps you want to begin having family devotions. Circle the letter before each phrase that describes what you will do.

a) Meet at home each day
b) Share needs and ask God for help
c) Include only the older children
d) Meet at the church once a week
e) Encourage each person to pray
f) Read from the Bible
g) Thank God for His blessings

Prayer: When to Pray

Prayer is one of the most important things a Christian can do. When you pray and God answers, you are working with God, so take time to pray.

- When you awake in the morning, begin the day with God and you will receive physical, moral, and spiritual strength for the problems of the day.

- Thank God for your food before eating.

- Have family devotions in the morning or evening.

- Take advantage of the times of prayer during church services and when you arrive before the service begins. Jesus said, "My house will be called a house of prayer" (Matthew 21:13).

- Lift your hearts to God at any time, thanking Him for His blessings or asking for His help. You do not always have to speak words when you talk to your Father this way; He knows your thoughts.

- Before you go to bed at night, thank God for His care during the day. Ask His forgiveness for anything wrong you have done, and entrust yourself to His care for the night.

Application

10 Use the list you have just read as a guide for prayer. Put a mark beside each of the suggested times for prayer that you want to add to what you are now doing.

Prayer: How to Pray

You may be saying to yourself, "But I don't know how to pray." Praying is not difficult. Just talk to God like you would to a friend. The Holy Spirit will help you.

Think about all that God has done for you, and thank Him for His blessings. Ask Him for your needs and those of your loved ones. Pray for the salvation of your friends and relatives. Pray for your pastor, your church, your brothers and sisters in Christ, and for God's work all over the world. Pray for new converts and their problems. Pray for your country. Just begin to pray, and you will soon learn how.

Jesus gave us a model that you may memorize and use in your prayers. This prayer is also referred to as the Lord's Prayer.

> This, then, is how you should pray: "Our Father in heaven, hallowed be your name, your kingdom come, your will be done on earth as it is in heaven. Give us today our daily bread. Forgive us our debts, as we also have forgiven our debtors. And lead us not into temptation, but deliver us from the evil one." (Matthew 6:9–13)

Application

11 Memorize the Lord's Prayer.

C. New Testimony

Goal 3. Choose to tell others about your faith in Jesus Christ.

Witnessing

To witness means to tell others what God has done for you. You can do this at home, on the street, in church services, or even by letter. Just as others spoke to you about Christ, you can speak to your friends and relatives. Pray for them to accept the Lord as Savior.

The Bible stresses the need of publicly declaring our faith in Christ, to let others know He is our Savior. Christ commanded the disciples to be witnesses. If you need courage, ask God for it, and He will give it to you. Thousands of people have been afraid to testify, just as you may be now, but they have conquered their fear and found great blessing and new strength in witnessing for Christ. The Lord Jesus said,

> Whoever acknowledges me before men, I will also acknowledge him before my Father in heaven. (Matthew 10:32)

> If anyone is ashamed of me and my words in this adulterous and sinful generation, the Son of Man will be ashamed of him when he comes in his Father's glory with the holy angels. (Mark 8:38)

Application

12 Following is a list of people you probably see often. Pray for them and ask God to help you share with them what Jesus has done for you.
a) Your family and your relatives
b) People with whom you work
c) Your friends
d) Your neighbors
e) Merchants in your community

Singing to the Lord

The ability to sing and make music is one of God's wonderful gifts to people. At home or at church, your songs will help, encourage, and bless you and others. It does not matter if your voice is not trained for singing; what matters is that you praise God from your heart.

> Let the word of Christ dwell in you richly as you teach and admonish one another with all wisdom, and as you sing psalms, hymns and spiritual songs with gratitude in your hearts to God. (Colossians 3:16)

Application

13 For a person to sing, the most important thing is for him or her to
a) have a pleasing voice.
b) be able to sing in front of others.
c) sing from the heart to glorify God.

D. NEW PARTNERSHIP

Goal 4. Identify ways you can partner with God.

Preaching the Gospel

Preaching the gospel is a very important activity of the church. Some are called to give their full time to this work. God gives them the responsibility of being pastors, evangelists, and missionaries.

Giving

Our Father is generous. As His children we must learn to act the way He does. This is the most important reason why we give. Giving to others is one way of showing that we belong to God. The money we give in church offerings helps many people. Some go to brothers and sisters who need clothing; some support the pastor in his or her duties as minister; and some pay for church expenses such as lights, water, and maintenance.

Our money can also be used to buy Bibles, equipment, and Christian literature. It can be used to pay for evangelistic radio and television programs. God has given His children the important work of telling others about salvation. By giving our money, we have a part in doing this important work.

The Bible describes a pattern of giving one-tenth of our income (called the "tithe") to the work of God. Many Christians follow this as a guide. They recognize that all they have comes from God, including the strength to earn money. In turn, they give back to God one tenth of what they earn. That tenth goes to support the church.

Christians who give generously discover the joy of becoming partners with God. At the same time, they find that their own needs are met. You can make these wonderful discoveries for yourself!

Jesus said, "Give, and it will be given to you" (Luke 6:38). Your giving brings three kinds of blessings:

1. Spiritual blessing. You become the kind of person God plans for you to become—generous to others.

2. Satisfaction. You are glad to be a dependable member of God's family, carrying your share of the load.

3. Security. God has promised to meet all your needs. As you obey Him, you can depend on Him to take care of you. Thousands of Christians can tell you from experience that God has never failed them.

> "Bring the whole tithe into the storehouse, that there may be food in my house. Test me in this," says the Lord Almighty, "and see if I will not throw open the floodgates of heaven and pour out so much blessing that you will not have room enough for it." (Malachi 3:10)

Each man should give what he has decided in his heart to give, not reluctantly or under compulsion, for God loves a cheerful giver. (2 Corinthians 9:7)

Application

14 Following are three statements about giving. Which one gives the most important reason Christians should give?
a) God is generous and gives good things to everyone.
b) Those who give will have their own needs met.
c) The tithe is one-tenth of God's earnings.

Helping in Any Way You Can

Whatever work you do for the Lord—from sweeping the chapel to holding a neighborhood service for a Sunday school in your home—will help you grow spiritually. Ask your pastor what you can do for the Lord.

Taking Part in Church Organization

There are many ways to get involved in church. For instance, go to Sunday school and small group meetings. There you can be a faithful member of one of the classes and study God's Word systematically. Do not miss this opportunity. The men, women, young people, and children may each have their own organizations. In their meetings they worship the Lord and carry out different projects for Him. Join one of these groups. You will receive a warm welcome and will enjoy its activities. These groups try to reach, teach, and help those who need it. Although one person can do very little, God working through His children united will carry His cause forward in this world.

Application

15 Here are some ways people take part in the church. Circle the letter before any you think you would like to do. Offer your services to the pastor or the leaders.

- **a)** Collecting or counting the offerings
- **b)** Caring for young children during worship services
- **c)** Visiting the sick and praying for them
- **d)** Helping older people come to the services
- **e)** Talking with those who have questions about what Christians believe
- **f)** Taking care of the church building and grounds
- **g)** Giving practical help to members who are in need
- **h)** Getting into a small group ministry
- **i)** Playing a musical instrument on the worship team
- **j)** Joining the choir
- **k)** Participating in evangelistic outreaches and events

Too Many Activities?

Do not worry if you cannot spend as much time in these activities as some people can. The Lord understands, and He will help you do what you can.

You will enjoy these activities of your new life. It will be satisfying to know you are helping others to escape eternal punishment and find eternal life. For everything you do for the Lord now, He will richly reward you in the world to come.

New Life, New Activities

Answers to Application Questions

7 c) forgive him or her and keep attending services.

1 b) their main interests.

8 Hebrews 10:25.

4 c) spend time with your heavenly Father.

9 Phrases **a)**, **b)**, **e)**, **f)**, and **g)** describe what you should do when you have family devotions.

5 a) explaining the way of salvation to others.

13 c) sing from the heart to glorify God.

6 An answer such as "encouraging each other" would be correct.

14 a) God is generous and gives good things to everyone.

UNIT ONE EVALUATION

Now that you have completed the first unit, you are ready to answer the *Unit One Evaluation*. Review the previous lessons before you begin. When you have completed the evaluation, check your answers using the answer key in the back of this book. Review the lesson material for any questions you answered incorrectly before continuing to Unit Two.

Lessons

6 Your New Standards
7 You Have a Helper
8 Your Life Is a Light
9 How to Have a Happy Home
10 Your New Freedom

LESSON 6 Your New Standards

In order to live together, people must follow certain rules or *standards*. Think about a family with several children. What would happen if the older ones were allowed to make noise all night? No one would get any rest. Therefore, standards are needed for everyday living.

Standards are also needed if a person wants to reach a special goal. Athletes, for example, follow the instructions of their coach. Their purpose is to develop skill and strength so they can win the prize. Now that you are a Christian, you have a new goal: to become all your heavenly Father wants you to be. This is another reason you need standards.

Your heavenly Father plans for you to be part of His family and reach the goals He has for your life. This lesson explains the new standards He has given to help you. Following them will bring you many benefits.

Lesson Outline

A. Who Sets the Standards?

B. Where Can You Find the Standards?

C. How Can You Meet the Standards?

D. Standards for Success

Lesson Goals

1. Describe the standards God has for you.

2. Explain how you can meet God's standards.

3. State the results that will come by meeting God's standards.

4. Describe successful living.

A. Who Sets the Standards?

Goal 1. Describe the standards God has for you.

In a home, parents set the standards on how their children should behave. The children soon learn that they must live by these standards. When they break the rules, their parents correct them. If they stubbornly refuse to obey, the parents may have to discipline them. Though the children are still members of the family, their disobedience brings them problems and suffering.

Our heavenly Father sets the standards for what His children should do and should not do. Sometimes He, too, has to discipline His children.

Application

1 The standards in a well-ordered home are set by the
- a) children.
- b) neighbors.
- c) parents.

2 The right to say how we should behave as Christians belongs to
a) our heavenly Father.
b) the culture in which we live.
c) us.

B. WHERE CAN YOU FIND THE STANDARDS?

Goal 2. Explain how you can meet God's standards.

We discover a person's standards by observing how he or she behaves. How do we find out the standards of a Christian? We discover the standards of a Christian by observing how Jesus Christ lived. The Bible gives us the record of His life. He is our perfect example and pattern for living.

We also discover Christian standards by studying what Jesus said about them. In the "Sermon on the Mount" (Matthew 5–7), Jesus described the standards of a Christian. These were His own standards. By His power working in us, they can become ours.

Jesus began His sermon by telling about the special blessings God gives to those who follow His standards. He continued with many other important teachings. Here are some of the things He said:

The Sermon on the Mount
Matthew 5–7

> Blessed are the poor in spirit, for theirs is the kingdom of heaven.
>
> Blessed are those who mourn, for they will be comforted.
>
> Blessed are the meek, for they will inherit the earth.
>
> Blessed are those who hunger and thirst for righteousness, for they will be filled.

Blessed are the merciful, for they will be shown mercy.

Blessed are the pure in heart, for they will see God.

Blessed are the peacemakers, for they will be called sons of God.

Blessed are those who are persecuted because of righteousness, for theirs is the kingdom of heaven.

You are the light of the world. . . . In the same way, let your light shine before men, that they may see your good deeds and praise your Father in heaven.

You have heard that it was said, "Eye for eye, and tooth for a tooth." But I tell you, do not resist an evil person.

You have heard that it was said, "Love your neighbor and hate your enemy." But I tell you: Love your enemies and pray for those who persecute you, that you may be sons of your Father in heaven.

Do not store up for yourselves treasures on earth, where moth and rust destroy, and where thieves break in and steal. But store up for yourselves treasures in heaven, where moth and rust do not destroy, and where thieves do not break in and steal. For where your treasure is, there your heart will be also.

So do not worry, saying, "What shall we eat?" or "What shall we drink?" or "What shall we wear?" For the pagans run after all these things, and your heavenly Father knows that you need them. But seek first his kingdom and his righteousness, and all these things will be given to you as well.

Application

3 The perfect pattern for your new life is found in
a) your pastor.
b) the saints of the church.
c) Jesus Christ.

4 Following are several opinions. Circle the letter in front of each one that matches Jesus' teaching in the verses you have read from the "Sermon on the Mount."
a) If another Christian is in need, I should help him or her and not keep all of my money for myself.
b) If someone tells lies about me, I have a right to hate that person.
c) If someone tries to rob me, I have a right to hit that person and injure him or her.
d) If I lose my job because I have become a Christian, I can be happy because God still cares for me.

Jesus gave us a basic principle for how to treat others. Many people call it the Golden Rule. "So in everything, do to others what you would have them do to you, for this sums up the Law and the Prophets" (Matthew 7:12).

Certainly we would all agree that people should not act badly toward others. Many religious leaders have said this. But the Golden Rule goes much further. Jesus is saying we should actively do good to others. We should be the first to treat them the way we ourselves would like to be treated.

We should not be proud, selfish, quarrelsome, or critical. We should not give place, even in our thoughts, to illicit love affairs or evil passions.

Our first interest should be to please God. We cannot make earthly riches our goal and serve God at the same time; but if we put Him first, He will see to it that all our needs are met. Besides, whatever we do for Him will be rewarded with eternal riches.

Application

5 Those who obey the Golden Rule most closely are those who
a) wait for others to do good to them, then do something good for them in return.
b) look for ways to do good to others.
c) find ways to get what they want for themselves.

6 Are there some ways you act that do not match Jesus' teachings? Underline each phrase that states a change you would like to make.
a) Forgive people who have mistreated you.
b) Give generously to those in need.
c) Pray for those who reject you because you are a Christian.
d) Think of good things to do for others and do them.
e) Work for peace in your family and community.

C. How Can You Meet the Standards?

Goal 3. State the results that will come by meeting God's standards.

Jesus knew that nobody would be able to follow these rules unless he or she had God's help. Therefore, He taught His disciples to ask their heavenly Father to help them. In Lesson 5, you learned about the model prayer—the Lord's Prayer. What help does God give you?

You can be like your heavenly Father because you share His life. How? Your Father has sent His Holy Spirit to live in you. This is how He has shared His own life with you. Do not worry about trying to live up to what God expects of you. He will help you. You will study more about this in the next lesson.

Application

7 Review the Lord's Prayer in Lesson 5. In this model prayer, Jesus taught us to pray to
a) the saints.
b) God, our heavenly Father.
c) our ancestors.

D. Standards for Success

Goal 4. Describe successful living.

Jesus lets us know that His instructions are the pattern for a successful life. Our life is like a building. Our thoughts, words, and actions are bricks in this building. As we line them up on the foundation of His teaching, we will have a character that can stand the tests of life.

Whoever lives as he or she pleases, without following the standards Jesus has given, will be a failure and will not be able to withstand the storms. If you want to be a successful Christian, build your life on Christ's teaching and follow His standards. The Holy Spirit will help you.

Application

8 Jesus teaches us that true success will come if we
a) build our lives on His teachings.
b) know what He said about happiness.
c) repeat many prayers every day.

Answers to Application Questions

4 a) If another Christian is in need, I should help him or her and not keep all of my money for myself.
  d) If I lose my job because I have become a Christian, I can be happy because God still cares for me

1 c) parents.

5 b) look for ways to do good to others.

2 a) our heavenly Father.

7 b) God, our heavenly Father.

3 c) Jesus Christ.

8 a) build our lives on His teachings.

LESSON 7
You Have a Helper

God never intended for you to live the Christian life without His help. In fact, God has come to actually live in you by the power of His Holy Spirit. You are not alone.

Some people think that becoming a Christian is just learning a new set of rules. They are wrong. The Christian life is not a set of rules you must keep. It does not depend on your struggles to be good. It is a new life from God, springing up inside you and flowing out from you.

As you let the Holy Spirit guide, you will learn how to keep God's standards. The Holy Spirit will give you power to turn away from evil and choose what is right. Daily, you will grow more like your heavenly Father.

Yes, you have a wonderful Helper! This lesson will explain who He is and how He helps you.

Lesson Outline

A. The Holy Spirit Is Your Helper

B. The Fruit of the Holy Spirit

C. Walking in the Holy Spirit

D. The Power of the Holy Spirit in You

E. The Gifts of the Holy Spirit

Lesson Goals

1. Identify the help God gives to you to live for Him.

2. Describe the different ways the Holy Spirit works in your life.

3. Experience personally the power of the Holy Spirit.

4. Describe the baptism in the Holy Spirit.

5. Identify truths about the gifts of the Holy Spirit.

A. THE HOLY SPIRIT IS YOUR HELPER

Goal 1. Identify the help God gives to you to live for Him.

Through the life and death of Jesus Christ, God provided everything for your salvation. He also has provided all you need to live your new life. He has done this by sending His Holy Spirit.

The Holy Spirit can be everywhere at once. When Jesus was on earth, He could be in only one place at a time. But after He ascended to heaven, He sent the Holy Spirit to be with all Christians—to live in us, guide us, and help us. John records Jesus's promise:

> I will ask the Father, and he will give you another Counselor to be with you forever. . . . But the Counselor, the Holy Spirit, whom the Father will send in my name, will teach you all things and will remind you of everything I have said to you. (John 14:16, 26)

Application

1 The Helper God has sent to be with you all the time is the
a) pastor of your church.
b) Holy Spirit. ✓
c) priest in your neighborhood.

2 The emphasis of the Christian life is on
a) obeying a set of rules.
b) your constant struggle to be good.
c) the Holy Spirit living in you. ✓

3 God's purpose in sending the Holy Spirit is to
a) live in you, guide you, and help you. ✓
b) take Jesus' place on earth.
c) be everywhere at once.

B. THE FRUIT OF THE HOLY SPIRIT

Goal 2. Describe the different ways the Holy Spirit works in your life.

The presence of the Holy Spirit in your life produces results that are called the fruit of the Spirit. He gives you the desire and strength to do the right thing. As you let Him lead and help you this way, He develops in you a Christian character. Your good attitudes, speech, and actions show you are a child of God. While your family and friends will enjoy being around you, most of all, this fruit of the Spirit pleases your heavenly Father.

> The fruit of the Spirit is love, joy, peace, patience, kindness, goodness, faithfulness, gentleness and self-control. Against such things there is no law. (Galatians 5:22–23)

> This is to my Father's glory, that you bear much fruit, showing yourselves to be my disciples. (John 15:8)

You Have a Helper 87

Application

4 The fruit of the Holy Spirit is the
a) people who hear the gospel message of Jesus Christ.
b) spiritual truth we find in the Bible.
c) good quality of character produced by the Spirit. ✓

5 Read Galatians 5:22–23 several times.

C. WALKING IN THE HOLY SPIRIT

Goal 3. Experience personally the power of the Holy Spirit.

It is natural for us to want to have our own way. This is a tendency of human nature. We want to do as we please instead of what is right. This is why we need to listen to the inner voice of the Holy Spirit as He urges us to do God's will and shows us the way. Galatians 5:16, 25 teaches, "So I say, live by the Spirit, and you will not gratify the desires of the sinful nature. . . . Let us not become conceited, provoking and envying each other."

God's Spirit will direct and strengthen you, but you must do your part. You must cooperate with the Holy Spirit and let Him guide you. This is what the Bible sometimes calls "walking in the Spirit." You are already doing this as you practice what you read in the Bible.

Application

6 According to Galatians 5:16, the "desires of the sinful nature" are those desires which lead us to
a) think only of ourselves and what we want. ✓
b) provide for the physical needs of our families.
c) improve our homes and surroundings.

D. THE POWER OF THE HOLY SPIRIT IN YOU

Goal 4. Describe the baptism in the Holy Spirit.

Jesus knew His followers would need a power greater than their own to do the work of God. He told them to wait until they were filled with the Holy Spirit to receive power to be His witnesses in all the world.

> On one occasion, while he was eating with them, he gave them this command: "Do not leave Jerusalem, but wait for the gift my Father promised, which you have heard me speak about. For John baptized with water, but in a few days you will be baptized with the Holy Spirit. . . . But you will receive power when the Holy Spirit comes on you; and you will be my witnesses in Jerusalem, and in all Judea and Samaria, and to the ends of the earth." (Acts 1:4–5, 8)

John the Baptist said this about Jesus: "I baptize you with water. But one more powerful than I will come, the thongs of whose sandals I am not worthy to untie. He will baptize you with the Holy Spirit and with fire" (Luke 3:16).

The book of Acts gives the thrilling story of how God fulfilled this promise on the Day of Pentecost and of the wonderful results afterwards.

> All of them were filled with the Holy Spirit and began to speak in other tongues as the Spirit enabled them. Now there were staying in Jerusalem God-fearing Jews from every nation under heaven. When they heard this sound, a crowd came together in bewilderment, because each one heard them speaking in his own language. Utterly amazed, they asked: "Are not all these men who are speaking Galileans? . . . (both Jews and converts to Judaism); Cretans and Arabs—we hear them

declaring the wonders of God in our own tongues!" (Acts 2:4–7, 11)

This baptism in the Holy Spirit, or infilling of the Holy Spirit, is also called the Pentecostal experience because it first occurred on the Day of Pentecost. When a person speaking under the power of the Holy Spirit uses a language he or she does not know, we sometimes call it *glossalalia*. This Greek word means "speaking in tongues." We also call it a *charismatic* experience, from *charisma*, which means "gift." This means it is a gift of the Holy Spirit and a supernatural experience.

Application

7 The baptism in the Holy Spirit most often refers to one's
a) being baptized by immersion in water.
b) bearing fruit according to Galatians 5:22–23.
c) speaking in tongues as described in Acts 2:4. ✓

8 On the Day of Pentecost, the Holy Spirit gave the disciples power to speak languages
a) no one knew.
b) they did not know.
c) had no meaning.

Speaking in tongues was the sign the Holy Spirit had come. But that was just the beginning. Jesus promised that the Holy Spirit would give us power. This power is for two purposes:

1. To help us tell others about Jesus.

2. To help us pray more effectively.

As Christians witness and pray in the power of the Holy Spirit, wonderful things take place, which can cause many people to turn to the Lord.

> Then Peter stood up with the Eleven, raised his voice and addressed the crowd: "Fellow Jews and all of you who live in Jerusalem, let me

explain this to you; listen carefully to what I say." (Acts 2:14)

Those who accepted his message were baptized, and about three thousand were added to their number that day. (Acts 2:41)

After they prayed, the place where they were meeting was shaken. And they were all filled with the Holy Spirit and spoke the word of God boldly. (Acts 4:31)

Application

9 The main purpose of the baptism in the Holy Spirit is to give Christians power to
a) witness and pray effectively. ✓
b) earn their salvation.
c) do miracles of healing.

This same power is for Christians today. Since the beginning of the twentieth century, several million people, in churches of different denominations all over the world, have enjoyed this Pentecostal experience in a baptism of power. In Acts 2:38–39, Peter preaches,

Repent and be baptized, every one of you, in the name of Jesus Christ for the forgiveness of your sins. And you will receive the gift of the Holy Spirit. The promise is for you and your children and for all who are far off—for all whom the Lord our God will call.

Application

10 Do you want this power of the Holy Spirit in your life? ....

Would you like to have the fire of God burning in you so that it will be easy to tell others about the Lord? ....

Do you want to pray more effectively? ....

This wonderful Pentecostal experience is for you. Ask God to baptize you with the Holy Spirit.

E. THE GIFTS OF THE HOLY SPIRIT

Goal 5. Identify truths about the gifts of the Holy Spirit.

As you have just read in Acts 2:38–39, the Holy Spirit himself is called a "gift." This word also points to the abilities He gives to Christians. The abilities are called "gifts" of the Holy Spirit. Christ wants His church to be full of spiritual power, so the Holy Spirit gives special abilities to different members. In this way, each person may have a part in the work and growth of the church. Paul writes to the church in Corinth, "There are different kinds of gifts, but the same Spirit . . . Now to each one the manifestation of the Spirit is given for the common good . . . All these are the work of one and the same Spirit, and he gives them to each one, just as he determines." (1 Corinthians 12:4, 7, 11).

Application

11 Following are several statements about the gifts of the Holy Spirit. Circle the letter before each one that is true.
a) All Christians have the same gifts.
b) Church leaders decide who will have which gift of the Holy Spirit.
c) A gift is given to one person, but all benefit when the gift is used.
d) All Christians can serve the Lord because all have a gift from the Holy Spirit.

12 Pray that God will continue the Pentecostal revival all over the world.

13 Ask the Holy Spirit to give you the gift of service that He wants you to have. Pray that He will give His gifts to other members of your church.

Answers to Application Questions

1 b) Holy Spirit.

7 c) speaking in tongues as described in Acts 2:4.

2 c) the Holy Spirit living in you.

8 b) they did not know.

3 a) live in you, guide you, and help you.

9 a) witness and pray effectively.

4 c) good quality of character produced by the Spirit.

11 Statements **c)** and **d)** are true.

6 a) think only of ourselves and what we want.

LESSON 8: Your Life Is a Light

The Bible teaches us that sin, error, and ignorance about God are like darkness. Everyone without Christ gropes along in this darkness—lost, deceived by Satan, and unable to find the way to heaven.

But God loves those in darkness! He sent His Son, Jesus Christ, to be the light of the world. Now that you have received Jesus, your life is full of light. His presence in you is like the flame of a candle or the power that makes a lamp shine. Because He is in you, you are God's candle, God's lamp. God wants the goodness and truth of Jesus to shine brightly through your life.

Many are watching you to see if what you say about the power of God is true. Your life shows them how the gospel can change people. What you do, even more than what you say, is a testimony for Jesus.

In this lesson, we will look at some of the rays of light that shine from your life because Jesus lives in you. These rays help convince others that the gospel is true.

Lesson Outline

A. Your Life as a Light
B. Eight Ways to Shine

Lesson Goals

1. Demonstrate God's light through your life.
2. Point out eight ways to bring good results in your life.

A. YOUR LIFE AS A LIGHT

Goal 1. Demonstrate God's light through your life.

You have learned that God sent His Son Jesus Christ to be the Light of the world. He did this because He loves all people and does not want anyone to be confused and fearful. This is what Jesus said: "I am the light of the world. Whoever follows me will never walk in darkness, but will have the light of life" (John 8:12).

Now that you are a Christian, the presence of Jesus Christ, the Light of the world, is in you. If it seems that you live in a dark place, do not be discouraged. God has placed you where you are as a lamp. Your life can show those around you the way to the Savior and heaven. Jesus taught,

> You are the light of the world. A city on a hill cannot be hidden. . . . In the same way, let your light shine before men, that they may see your good deeds and praise your Father in heaven. (Matthew 5:14, 16)

Application

1 Read John 8:12 and complete this sentence: The person who has the light of life is one who ....
....

2 Your life can be a light because you
a) are talented with brilliant ideas.
b) have the presence of Jesus in you.
c) attend the meetings of the local church.

3 Following are several questions. Write your answer to each one in the space provided.
a) Do you know anyone whose life has made you want to follow Jesus? ....
b) Do you want to be a lamp for the Lord?. ....
c) As a lamp for the Lord, are you willing to let Him take you wherever the darkness is greatest so your light will shine there?. ....
d) Will you pray each day that the Lord will use your life to show others the way to heaven?. ....

People need to hear preaching about Jesus. But they also need to see Christians in action. Your life can be a powerful, living sermon that convinces others of the truth of the gospel. Let us study eight rays of light that can shine from you each day.

B. Eight Ways to Shine

Goal 2. Point out eight ways to bring good results in your life.

Be Honest

Paying your bills promptly is a good testimony. Christians should be fair and honest in all their business dealings. They should pay back promptly or return in good condition whatever they borrow. They should not take on financial obligations they are unable to meet. They should keep their promises.

> Do not repay anyone evil for evil. Be careful to do what is right in the eyes of everybody. (Romans 12:17)

> Give everyone what you owe him: If you owe taxes, pay taxes; if revenue, then revenue; if respect, then respect; if honor, then honor. Let no debt remain outstanding, except the continuing debt to love one another, for he who loves his fellowman has fulfilled the law. (Romans 13:7–8)

Application

4 Do you have any debts you need to pay? Describe what you will do to make things right.

....

Talk Like a Child of God

What would people think of God's power to save if you cursed and swore or told dirty stories? Would your light shine for God if you quarreled, gossiped, criticized others, bragged on yourself, told lies, and used harsh, coarse language?

On the other hand, many people have been convinced of the power of the gospel by the changed talk of those who become Christians. One of the hardest things for anybody to do is to control his or her tongue. Not only what you say but your very tone of voice can either help draw people to Christ or turn them against Christianity. James 1:26 warns, "If anyone considers himself religious and yet does not keep a tight rein on his tongue, he deceives himself and his religion is worthless."

Application

5 Ask yourself these questions: "Does the way I talk make people feel the love of God? Or do I offend people? What changes do I need to make in the things I say?"

6 Each day, ask Jesus to help you talk like a child of God should. Here is a verse from the Bible you can use as a prayer.

> May the words of my mouth and the meditation of my heart be pleasing in your sight, O Lord, my Rock and my Redeemer. (Psalm 19:14)

Help Others

If we really love our neighbors as ourselves, we will show it in practical ways by helping those who need our help. Ask God to show you how you can be a real friend to those who have problems and troubles. "Religion that God our Father accepts as pure and faultless is this: to look after orphans and widows in their distress and to keep oneself from being polluted by the world" (James 1:27).

Application

7 Following are ways of showing care and concern for others. In the spaces given, write the names of people you could help in these ways, or describe something else you could do for someone you know.

- Visiting a sick person
- Visiting someone in prison
- Donating food to someone who is unemployed
- Helping someone find a job
- Helping someone get to a church service
- Helping a handicapped person shop or clean

- Making household repairs
- ....
- ....
- ....

Act Wisely

"Avoid every kind of evil" (1 Thessalonians 5:22). Foolish actions can ruin a person's influence for God. For example, showing love to our Christian brothers and sisters is a wonderful thing. But we should not act in ways that give the wrong impression. How do other people interpret what you do? Act wisely. Be a good example in all you do, and your light will shine brightly for God.

> Do not allow what you consider good to be spoken of as evil. (Romans 14:16)

> Don't let anyone look down on you because you are young, but set an example for the believers in speech, in life, in love, in faith and in purity. (1 Timothy 4:12)

Application

8 Suppose you meet a young person who wants to know more about Christianity. This person's parents are not Christians. The young person asks to meet you late at night to discuss the Bible. In order to act wisely, what should you do? Write your answer in your notebook.

Stay Healthy

A Christian should observe the rules of hygiene, setting an example of cleanliness in his or her home, clothing, and person. But cleanliness goes further than that. Your body is the temple of the Holy Spirit; therefore, you ought to keep it clean inside and outside. Your body should not be soiled, weakened, or made sick by any vice or immoral act. Keep your body strong and healthy so you can work for the Lord.

It is a well-known fact that smoking cigarettes is one of the principal causes of lung cancer and causes many deaths. Also, alcoholism and drugs kill thousands every year. We must not commit suicide, either instantly or gradually, because this would also destroy God's temple.

> Don't you know that you yourselves are God's temple and that God's Spirit lives in you? If anyone destroys God's temple, God will destroy him; for God's temple is sacred, and you are that temple. (1 Corinthians 3:16–17)

The Bible prohibits drunkenness. Notice what it commands: "Do not get drunk on wine, which leads to debauchery. Instead, be filled with the Spirit" (Ephesians 5:18). You can show reverence for God by treating the body He has given you with respect. Practice habits that lead to good health, and avoid those that bring harm. You will be rewarded in two ways. You will have the physical well-being that comes from treating your body right and the spiritual joy that comes from obeying God.

Application

9 Listed are habits that affect your body. Underline those that lead to good health.

cleanliness	proper exercise
drug addiction	proper rest
drunkenness	sensible eating
overeating	using tobacco

Jesus came to bring you freedom and well-being in all areas of your life. If you have a problem with any bad habit, talk with your pastor. Ask him or her and the church to pray for you so you will get complete victory. Your changed life will be a testimony to others whom you wish to see freed from the chains of sin and vice.

Application

10 If a Christian is having a hard time getting rid of bad habits, he or she should
a) give up going to church.
b) practice the habits in secret.
c) ask for special prayer.

Behave Modestly

We should be modest in our speech, actions, and appearance. Modesty is the opposite of pride and vanity. If we act like we are better than others and look down on people who do things we would not do, we will drive them away from Christianity instead of winning them for the Lord.

We have absolutely no right to be proud about who we are, what we do, or what we have. We do not deserve a thing God has done for us or given us. If it were not for His mercy and work in our lives, we might be the most wretched, horrible sinners the world has ever known.

Vain, proud people want everyone to notice them. They may call attention to themselves through fashion fads, expensive clothing and jewelry, or by showing off their superior knowledge and abilities. They may try to make people notice them by going against approved customs of dress and conduct. A proud person may even boast of his or her spiritual experience and consecration to the Lord. Modest people are not like that. They do not try to call attention to themselves. A modest Christian avoids styles that are extreme, indecent, or in bad taste for the children of the Lord.

Several passages in the Bible urge modesty and warn against vanity. All of us have a desire to look nice, and we can be tempted to pay more attention to how we look. Of course, God is not against beauty. But He wants our beauty to come from the inside—from a beautiful character that shines through in a pleasant, joyful face. Peter says beauty should "be that of your inner self, the unfading beauty of a gentle and quiet spirit, which is of great worth in God's sight" (1 Peter 3:4).

Application

11 Modest behavior is valuable because it
a) allows our inner beauty to shine through.
b) shows others we have a low opinion of ourselves.
c) makes us more holy in God's sight.

Accept Responsibility

We have to earn our living by honest work and not let the love of money take us into such things as gambling, lottery, or any game of chance. We do not produce or sell things that harm others. "For the love of money is a root of all kinds of evil. Some people, eager for money, have wandered from the faith and pierced themselves with many griefs" (1 Timothy 6:10).

God wants us to be good workers, not lazy people. Honest work brings many benefits. Those who accept responsibility for themselves and their families gain self-respect. They also gain the respect of their employers. Christians who have done their work well, without complaining, have convinced more than one manager that the gospel is real.

When the church first began, Christians often ate together. However, some came to eat who did not want to work. The leaders had this rule:

> If a man will not work, he shall not eat.
> (2 Thessalonians 3:10)

> Make it your ambition to lead a quiet life, to mind your own business and to work with your hands, just as we told you, so that your daily

life may win the respect of outsiders and so that you will not be dependent on anybody.
(1 Thessalonians 4:11–12)

If you cannot find a job, tell your pastor and your Christian brothers and sisters. Ask for prayer, and be willing to do any kind of honest work. God knows your needs, and He will help you.

Application

12 Circle the letter in front of each sentence that describes the Christian view of work.
a) Work is not necessary because God will provide.
b) Any way a person can earn money is all right.
c) Honest, good work is a duty and a testimony.
d) If someone else will support you, you do not need to work.

Treat Your Family Right

How do you treat your family? Your home life speaks loudly to others—for good or bad. Many have lost interest in the gospel because of quarrels in the homes of people who call themselves Christians. On the other hand, many who had little interest in preaching have been won to Christ by seeing the patience, love, and joy of the Lord in a Christian home. You will study more about this in the next lesson.

Application

13 Following are the eight practical ways you can be a light in your community. Circle the letters before those you most need to begin doing right away. Ask God to help you with each one.
a) Be honest.
b) Talk like a child of God.
c) Help others.
d) Act wisely.
e) Stay healthy.
f) Behave modestly.
g) Accept responsibility.
h) Treat your family right.

Answers to Application Questions

10 c) ask for special prayer.

1 follows Jesus.

11 a) allows our inner beauty to shine through.

2 b) have the presence of Jesus in you.

12 c) Honest, good work is a duty and a testimony.

9 Those that lead to good health are cleanliness, proper exercise, proper rest, and sensible eating. Did you notice that most bad habits are expensive? When a person is free from them, the money saved is an extra reward.

LESSON 9
How to Have a Happy Home

The Bible teaches that God created the family. He planned for the man and woman to live together as husband and wife and to bring children into the world. Because He did, we can depend on Him to help our families.

God helps us by being present in our homes. In a Christian home, Christ is the Head. His presence fills it with joy, peace, and love.

God also helps by giving us guidelines to follow for family living. These guidelines help people know how to act as husbands and wives and how to behave as parents and children. In this lesson, you will study these guidelines.

There is no greater blessing in this world than having a home that is truly Christian. It is a shelter from the storms of sin and trouble. It is a place where children feel secure and loved. You can make your home a little bit of heaven if you do as God tells you!

How to Have a Happy Home

Lesson Outline

A. Pray for Your Family's Salvation

B. Be a Good Christian at Home

C. Keep Marriage Sacred

D. Follow God's Pattern for Family Living

Lesson Goals

1. Know how to pray for your family.

2. Describe how to live for Christ at home.

3. Indicate ways to improve your marriage.

4. Show how to build a strong, happy family life.

A. PRAY FOR YOUR FAMILY'S SALVATION

Goal 1. Know how to pray for your family.

You can pray in faith knowing that your family's salvation is the will of God. Do not be discouraged if your family does not get saved immediately. Keep on praying; God will answer prayer. "Believe in the Lord Jesus, and you will be saved—you and your household" (Acts 16:31).

Application

1 Your home can be a little bit of heaven on earth if you
a) have enough money to furnish it well.
b) invite a lot of people in to visit.
c) follow God's rules for family living.

2 If the other members of your family do not become Christians immediately, you should
a) keep on praying for them.
b) stop praying for them.
c) think that God will not save them.

3 Pray now for every member of your immediate family. Make a habit of praying for them every day.

B. Be a Good Christian at Home

Goal 2. Describe how to live for Christ at home.

It is easy to act like a good Christian in church, but what kind of a Christian are you at home?

Read the following instructions from the Bible. Think of how you measure up to these teachings at home.

> But now you must rid yourselves of all such things as these: anger, rage, malice, slander, and filthy language from your lips. Do not lie to each other, since you have taken off your old self with its practices. (Colossians 3:8–9)

> Therefore, as God's chosen people, holy and dearly loved, clothe yourselves with compassion, kindness, humility, gentleness and patience. Bear with each other and forgive whatever grievances you may have against one another. Forgive as the Lord forgave you. And over all these virtues put on love, which binds them all together in perfect unity. (Colossians 3:12–14)

Do you show appreciation for the work of your wife or husband? For the help of your children or brothers and sisters? For the sacrifices your parents have made for you?

Are you loving or selfish? Are you cross and irritable or patient and forgiving? Are you dictatorial, or do you listen to the opinions of others? Are you respectful and obedient to your parents or willful and disobedient?

Are you helpful and obliging, or are you lazy? Do you gladly cooperate with others without criticizing and complaining? Do you become discouraged easily, or are you cheerful when things go wrong? Do others find it easy to live with you?

Application

4 If you want to have a happy home, humbly admit your failings. Then ask the Lord to help you overcome them. If you are willing to do your part, He will help you.

Ask Forgiveness for Your Wrongs

Jesus taught us to ask forgiveness of those whom we have wronged. If you are not willing to do this, it will stand in the way of your fellowship with God.

> Therefore, if you are offering your gift at the altar and there remember that your brother has something against you, leave your gift there in front of the altar. First go and be reconciled to your brother; then come and offer your gift. (Matthew 5:23–24)

Apologizing for wrongdoing is not always easy, but it is a good way to get rid of hard feelings and keep your home happy. Do you have a bad disposition? Acknowledging your fault and asking your loved ones to pray for you is a long step toward victory. "Therefore confess your sins to each other and pray for each other so that you may be healed. The prayer of a righteous man is powerful and effective" (James 5:16).

Application

5 Your home will be happier if you
a) make everyone who has been unkind to you ask your forgiveness.
b) ask forgiveness when you have acted unkindly toward someone in your family.
c) show everyone you are the boss and make them afraid of you.

6 Read James 5:16 several times.

Be Cheerful

Have faith in God and praise Him for the answers to your prayers, even when everything looks dark. Nehemiah said, "Go and enjoy choice food and sweet drinks, and send some to those who have nothing prepared. This day is sacred to our Lord. Do not grieve, for the joy of the Lord is your strength" (Nehemiah 8:10).

Do not be discouraged if you have a hard time controlling your temper or some other disagreeable trait in your character. The very effort you are making to overcome it is a testimony of your love for the Lord. He is helping you grow spiritually. Does your growth seem too slow? Look more to the Lord and less to yourself, and you will be surprised how He will solve the problems in your home. God is your loving Father who cares for you.

Application

7 Think over the way you treat the people in your family. What change do you most need to make?

....

Ask God to help you make this change, and keep asking.

C. KEEP MARRIAGE SACRED

Goal 3. Indicate ways to improve your marriage.

God wants you to have a happy home. His Word gives guidelines to help make your marriage happy.

> At the beginning of creation God "made them male and female." "For this reason a man will leave his father and mother and be united to his wife, and the two will become one flesh." So they are no longer two, but one. Therefore what

> God has joined together, let man not separate.
> (Mark 10:6–9)

Many couples today live together without getting married. When a person becomes a Christian, he or she will want to have a legal marriage. In this way, the couple has a better testimony in the community, gives protection of the laws of the land to their family, and honors Christ. If you should need advice about the necessary legal documents, talk with your pastor about it. He or she will be happy to help you.

> Do not repay anyone evil for evil. Be careful
> to do what is right in the eyes of everybody.
> (Romans 12:17)

> Live such good lives among the pagans that,
> though they accuse you of doing wrong, they
> may see your good deeds and glorify God on the
> day he visits us. (1 Peter 2:12)

God's Word takes a strong stand against any kind of sexual relations outside of marriage. It strictly prohibits any flirtation or illicit love affair by either partner with another person. Hebrews 13:4 warns, "Marriage should be honored by all, and the marriage bed kept pure, for God will judge the adulterer and all the sexually immoral."

Couples who keep their marriage vows enjoy great blessings. They can trust each other because they know each is faithful to the other in thought, word, and deed. As they serve the Lord together, their marriage reflects the life of heaven. It is free from the deception, suspicion, jealousy, and unfaithfulness that wreck so many homes.

Application

8 Following are some ideas about marriage. Circle the letter before each one that agrees with Christian teachings.

a) A couple should live together before marriage to see if they are suited for one another.

b) The legal ceremony of marriage is unnecessary for people who really love each other.

c) A couple who wishes to show honor for each other and for God will be legally married.

d) Love affairs outside of marriage are acceptable as long as they are kept secret.

You can depend on God to help you in your marriage. Pray that His love will strengthen your love for each other. Thank Him for your partner. Pray that He will help you keep your marriage vows in thought, word, and deed. Ask God to help you trust each other.

Marry a Christian

You have accepted Christ as the Master of your life. If your husband or wife does not want to serve Him, you will find yourselves going in opposite directions. You will always be torn between the desire to please Christ in everything and the desire to please your companion.

As a Christian you want to please God. You want to be useful to Him, attend church services, enjoy fellowship with other Christians, and take part in the work of the church. You would like to have family prayer at home, praising and serving God together as a family.

The unsaved husband or wife is not interested in these things. Sometimes if your spouse goes with you to church, he or she feels you should go with him or her to places of amusement that are not good for a Christian. Or else your spouse goes one way, and you go another, making your home unhappy. Worse still, many Christians have let an unsaved companion turn them away from the Lord.

God does not want you to fall into a trap that Satan uses on so many Christians. God's Word warns against marrying an unbeliever. The following verse applies to your choice of a husband or wife: "Do not be yoked together with unbelievers. For what do righteousness and wickedness have in common? Or what fellowship can light have with darkness?" (2 Corinthians 6:14).

If you marry someone of a different religion, there will be grave problems. How can you agree on religious training for the children? How can you bring them up to serve the Lord?

Of course, if you are already married to someone who is not a true Christian, your duty is to pray and try to win him or her to Christ. You are to be a faithful wife or husband and let your light shine for God in your home. But if you are still single and are going to get married, be sure to marry a Christian. This is the only way you can have real unity and peace in your family life.

Application

9 Suppose you have a Christian friend who has a non-Christian sweetheart. Your friend asks you what the Bible says about marrying non-Christians. What should you answer?

D. FOLLOW GOD'S PATTERN FOR FAMILY LIVING

Goal 4. Show how to build a strong, happy family life.

Be a Good Parent

Parents are responsible to God for taking good care of their children. They should provide for the material and spiritual needs of their family. They should give the children the loving care they need. Church activities do not free parents from their responsibilities to their family. "If anyone does not provide for his relatives, and especially for his immediate family, he has denied the faith and is worse than an unbeliever" (1 Timothy 5:8).

Teach Your Children to Love God

If you teach your children to love God and obey His Word when they are small, you will save them and yourself many heartaches when they are older. Gather the family for a time with God in Bible reading and prayer each day. Let each one take part. Pray together over the problems of each member of the family. Thank God together for His blessings.

Go to Sunday school and church together. Encourage your children to give their lives to God at an early age. As you worship and serve God together, His love strengthens family ties. As the saying goes, "The family that prays together stays together." Paul writes, "Fathers, do not exasperate your children; instead, bring them up in the training and instruction of the Lord" (Ephesians 6:4).

Love Your Family

God is love. The more of God you have in your life, the more love you will have for your family. And the more love you have in your home, the happier it will be. When your children need correction, you should discipline them because of your love for them rather than in anger.

> Love is patient, love is kind. It does not envy, it does not boast, it is not proud. It is not rude, it is not self-seeking, it is not easily angered, it keeps no record of wrongs. Love does not delight in evil but rejoices with the truth. It always protects, always trusts, always hopes, always perseveres. (1 Corinthians 13:4–7)

Application

10 Circle the letter in front of each example of God's pattern for family living.
a) John feels called to preach. He abandons his wife and children and travels as an evangelist.
b) Martha expects the church leaders to do all the work of teaching her children about God.
c) Tom and Susan read the Bible to their children and pray with them each day.
d) William disciplines his children fairly. He makes sure they understand what he expects of them.

If you are a parent, pray for each of your children now. Ask the Lord to help you be patient and understanding. Pray that all your family members will love each other more.

Answers to Application Questions

8 Only statement **c)** agrees with Christian teachings.

1 c) follow God's rules for family living.

9 You should answer that 2 Corinthians 6:14 tells believers not to try to work together with unbelievers. A Christian who marries a non-Christian is disobeying this command. You should also encourage your friend to pray about this problem, asking God to bring him or her a Christian marriage partner.

2 a) keep on praying for them.

10 c) Tom and Susan read the Bible to their children and pray with them each day.
  d) William disciplines his children fairly. He makes sure they understand what he expects of them.

5 b) ask forgiveness when you have acted unkindly toward someone in your family.

LESSON 10 Your New Freedom

Most people want freedom. Some want freedom from oppressive laws and harsh dictators. Still others want the freedom to say and do anything they please. But what is real freedom? Can a person in prison be free? Can someone in an unjust society be free?

The answer is yes. True freedom is not what is outside a person, but what is inside. In the Bible, Paul the apostle writes about "the glorious freedom of the children of God" (Romans 8:21). Only the children of God have true freedom.

This lesson discusses the freedom you have now because you are a child of God. This liberty sets you free from the terrible effects of sin. It liberates you from the fear that you will not be able to please God. It helps you overcome spiritual error and confusion. These blessings are yours because of what Jesus Christ has done for you. But they are just the beginning. Your new life of freedom will continue into eternity!

Lesson Outline

A. Freedom from Sin

B. Freedom from Fear

C. Freedom from Error

D. Freedom from Confusion

E. Freedom from Worry

F. Freedom in the Future

Lesson Goal

1. Describe the freedom you have as a child of God, both now and in the future.

A. Freedom from Sin

Goal   Describe the freedom you have as a child of God, both now and in the future.

Jesus died to set you free from the guilt, punishment, power, and presence of sin.

- *Guilt*: He took the blame for everything wrong you have ever done.

- *Punishment*: You were condemned to die, but Jesus died in your place. By accepting Him as your Savior, you are free from the death sentence.

- *Power*: Jesus conquered Satan and broke sin's power over you.

> Anyone who has died has been freed from sin. Now if we died with Christ, we believe that we will also live with him. (Romans 6:7–8)

> In the same way, count yourselves dead to sin but alive to God in Christ Jesus. (Romans 6:11)

> Now that you have been set free from sin and have become slaves to God, the benefit you reap leads to holiness, and the result is eternal life. (Romans 6:22)
>
> Therefore, there is now no condemnation for those who are in Christ Jesus. (Romans 8:1)

Application

1 You are set free from the guilt, punishment, and power of sin by
a) doing penance for your sins.
b) deciding to be good from now on.
c) accepting Jesus as your Savior.

- *Temptation to sin*: Some people are delivered instantly from their bad habits the moment they accept the Lord. Others fight for months or years against their craving for tobacco, drugs, or other vices; but as they keep on praying and believing, God gives them victory.

> So if the Son sets you free, you will be free indeed. (John 8:36)

> Submit yourselves, then, to God. Resist the devil, and he will flee from you. (James 4:7)

If you still have a battle against bad habits, do not give up. When the devil tempts you, claim by faith the freedom that Christ gives. Begin to praise the Lord for freedom, and you will soon get victory over the tempter. Your pastor will be glad to pray with you and help you.

You will face different kinds of temptation while you live on this earth. But these temptations are tests that will help you grow. You will become stronger each time you resist them. When you get to heaven, God's work in you will be complete: you will be forever free from any desire to sin.

Application

2 Read John 8:36 and James 4:7 carefully.

3 Based on James 4:7, which statement is true?
a) The devil will defeat you if you try to resist him.
b) If you oppose the devil, he will go away from you.
c) The devil is not affected by what you do.

- *Effects and presence of sin*: Now you see sin and its effects all around you—suffering, sorrow, and death. Some glorious day you will go to your eternal home and be free from even the memory of sin.

Application

4 Following are several kinds of freedom from sin. Match the phrase (right) to each kind of freedom it describes (left).

.... **a)** Freedom from the guilt of sin

.... **b)** Freedom from all the effects of sin

.... **c)** Freedom from the power of sin

.... **d)** Freedom from the punishment of sin

.... **e)** Freedom from the presence of sin

1) Freedom now and in the future
2) Freedom in the future

5 Now that you are a Christian, why does God still allow you to be tempted to sin?

....

B. Freedom from Fear

You are free from the fear of what others may do to you. Your life is under God's care, "hidden with Christ in God" (Colossians 3:3). You may have to suffer for Christ's sake or even die, but He will be with you every moment. Nothing can happen to you except what He permits. Paul writes, "If God is for us, who can be against us?" (Romans 8:31).

You are free from the fear of witchcraft, the evil eye, and the fear of bad luck. With the living Christ at your side to protect you, you do not need to use medallions, fetishes, jujus, a glass of water before a picture, a charm on your child's wrist or neck, a picture of a guardian angel, or any other image to protect you. God is not pleased with your trusting in these things. He promises to protect you.

> God has said, "Never will I leave you; never will I forsake you." So we say with confidence, "The Lord is my helper; I will not be afraid. What can man do to me?" (Hebrews 13:5–6)

> You, dear children, are from God and have overcome them, because the one who is in you is greater than the one who is in the world. (1 John 4:4)

Application

6 The best way to be free from fear is to
a) use strong magic.
b) trust in the Lord.
c) light candles to an image.

C. Freedom from Error

Satan has trapped millions of people in false religions. He gives them mistaken ideas of how to get to heaven. They pray to the sun and the moon, to rocks, rivers, and trees, and try to find the truth in dreams and revelations. They ask the spirits of the dead to help them. They burn candles and incense to idols made of gold, silver, wood, stone, or plaster. They offer sacrifices and make vows as they pray to spirits for help.

God's Word—not human ideas—shows us the true way to heaven. As you read God's Word, you discover the truth and are free from these errors. John 8:31–32 records, "To the Jews who had believed him, Jesus said, 'If you hold to my teaching, you are really my disciples. Then you will know the truth, and the truth will set you free.'"

Application

7 We are set free from error by the
a) revelations we receive in dreams.
b) ideas of other people about heaven.
c) truth we learn in the Bible.

In the following Bible verses, God strongly opposes the use of images and any form of spiritism. Now that you have given your life to Him, His commands are more important than any vows you may have made to idols. These commands are from God. He has the power to free you from promises you have made to any images, spirits, or false gods.

> You shall have no other gods before me. "You shall not make for yourself an idol in the form of anything in heaven above or on the earth beneath or in the waters below. You shall not bow down to them or worship them; for I, the Lord your God, am a jealous God, punishing the children for the sin of the fathers to the third and fourth generation of those who hate me." (Exodus 20:3–5)

> Let no one be found among you who sacrifices his son or daughter in the fire, who practices divination or sorcery, interprets omens, engages in witchcraft, or casts spells, or who is a medium or spiritist or who consults the dead. Anyone who does these things is detestable to the Lord, and because of these detestable practices the

Lord your God will drive out those nations before you. (Deuteronomy 18:10–12)

You are free from serving any spirits or false gods because you now belong to the one true God. You are also free from the power of evil spirits and from fear of what they might do to you. God's Holy Spirit who lives in your heart is more powerful than any evil spirits that seek to torment you.

Application

8 Have you practiced or believed any of the errors listed in this lesson or in the verses from the Bible? If so, pray the following prayer. Name all the practices that you now forsake. Ask God to set you free from them and any fear you may have because of them.

Heavenly Father, You are the only true God. You are greater than anything in heaven or earth. I turn away from

. . . .

. . . .

and will never practice those things again. I will worship You alone, through Jesus Christ Your only Son, my Lord and Savior.

D. Freedom from Confusion

In the Old Testament of the Bible, there are many laws. Some people are confused about what these laws mean for us today.

Many of these laws are ceremonial in nature and belong to a covenant God made with the Hebrews many years ago. Moses received the terms of this covenant and all its rules for the new nation that he had led out of Egypt. The laws included instructions about sacrifices, holy days, forms of worship, cleanliness, and food. Some call this covenant the "Mosaic" law, naming it after Moses.

All these religious regulations were like pictures of Jesus Christ and the salvation He would provide. He would be the perfect sacrifice who would take away our sins. He would fulfill all the Law stood for and establish a new covenant with those who accept Him as Savior, whether they were Hebrews or not.

The restrictions in the Mosaic law were for the Hebrews from the time of Moses to the time of Christ on earth. Since then, we are under the terms of the new covenant, the New Testament.

Application

9 The time period of the Mosaic law is from the
a) beginning of the world until Moses.
b) time of Moses until the time of Christ on earth.
c) time of Christ's birth until now.

Some people get confused and think we have to keep Saturday as a holy day, as the Mosaic law required. But ever since Jesus rose from the dead on the first day of the week, Christians have had the custom of meeting on that day, Sunday, in memory of His resurrection. Since Bible times, they have called it "the Lord's Day".

Today, we set aside one day a week as a time to meet together to worship God. However, we do this not because of any rules or obligations. We do this because we love God and because the Holy Spirit gives us a desire to be with our brothers and sisters in the Lord.

Under the Mosaic law the people could not eat certain animals. Under the new covenant we are not bound by these restrictions. We have the same freedom God gave humanity long before the Mosaic law. He told Noah that humans were not to eat blood, and this prohibition is repeated in the New Testament. But we can eat any kind of meat.

> Everything that lives and moves will be food for you. Just as I gave you the green plants, I now

> give you everything. But you must not eat meat that has its lifeblood still in it. (Genesis 9:3–4)

> For everything God created is good, and nothing is to be rejected if it is received with thanksgiving, because it is consecrated by the word of God and prayer. (1 Timothy 4:4–5)

> Eat anything sold in the meat market without raising questions of conscience . . . If some unbeliever invites you to a meal and you want to go, eat whatever is put before you without raising questions of conscience. (1 Corinthians 10:25, 27)

> Therefore do not let anyone judge you by what you eat or drink, or with regard to a religious festival, a New Moon celebration or a Sabbath day. (Colossians 2:16)

Application

10 Circle the letter before each true statement.
a) The religious regulations of the Mosaic law were pictures of the perfect sacrifice, Jesus Christ.
b) Christians today must worship God on the seventh day of the week (Saturday).
c) Christians today are free to eat any kind of meat.
d) Rules about holy days apply to Christians today.

E. Freedom from Worry

Your Father loves you and will take care of your needs. Trust in Him.

> Cast all your anxiety on him because he cares for you. (1 Peter 5:7)

> So do not worry, saying, "What shall we eat?" or "What shall we drink?" or "What shall we

wear?" For the pagans run after all these things, and your heavenly Father knows that you need them. But seek first his kingdom and his righteousness, and all these things will be given to you as well. (Matthew 6:31–33)

Application

11 Read 1 Peter 5:7 again. Are you worrying about anything? Tell your heavenly Father about it. Thank Him for the answer.

Sickness brings worry and anxiety into our lives. But this is another kind of worry we can leave with our heavenly Father. Jesus Christ, the Great Physician, is your best friend. He loves you. Just as He healed the sick when He was here on earth, He heals people today in answer to prayer. The Bible says you should ask for the church elders (the pastor and the leaders) to pray for you when you are sick.

> Is any one of you sick? He should call the elders of the church to pray over him and anoint him with oil in the name of the Lord. And the prayer offered in faith will make the sick person well; the Lord will raise him up. If he has sinned, he will be forgiven. (James 5:14–15)

The pastor and the elders may put their hands on you, or they may ask God to touch and heal you. Or they may anoint you with oil; this is a way of showing they trust in the power of the Holy Spirit to make you well.

Application

12 Do you need healing? Ask your pastor to pray for you. If you are studying by correspondence, the workers at the school will be glad to pray for you. Write them about your need when you send in your answer sheet.

Many people have had wonderful healings from God. But sometimes God chooses not to heal a person right away. For example, the apostle Paul prayed to God three times about a certain problem. God heard Paul's prayer, but God did not remove the problem. He said to Paul, "My grace is sufficient for you, for my power is made perfect in weakness" (2 Corinthians 12:9).

Whatever happens, though, you can trust God completely. One day He will change your body into one like that of the Lord Jesus. Your new body will be perfect! No disease, sickness, deformity, or weakness will ever cause trouble for you again.

F. Freedom in the Future

The freedom you have is wonderful. But God has much more planned for the future. Jesus, the great liberator, will return to earth for those who belong to Him. At that time you will know, at last, the full and glorious freedom of the children of God. Jesus will take you to your heavenly home. The whole creation will be set free forever from the presence and effects of sin.

> He will wipe every tear from their eyes. There will be no more death or mourning or crying or pain, for the old order of things has passed away. (Revelation 21:4)

> I consider that our present sufferings are not worth comparing with the glory that will be revealed in us. (Romans 8:18)

> For the creation was subjected to frustration, not by its own choice, but by the will of the one who subjected it, in hope that the creation itself will be liberated from its bondage to decay and brought into the glorious freedom of the children of God. (Romans 8:20–21)

Application

13 Read Revelation 21:4. Thank God for His message and for the glorious future He has planned for you.

Until Jesus comes to take us home, we will still have to battle against Satan. There will be temptations and trials, but we must not give up our freedom. Galatians 5:1 reminds us, "It is for freedom that Christ has set us free. Stand firm, then, and do not let yourselves be burdened again by a yoke of slavery."

Never forget that your new life and freedom are in the Lord Jesus Christ. They depend on His presence and His power in you—not on how good you try to be. The Christian life is not about keeping a set of rules. It is about demonstrating "Christ in you, the hope of glory" (Colossians 1:27).

> Therefore, if anyone is in Christ, he is a new creation; the old has gone, the new has come! (2 Corinthians 5:17)

> I have been crucified with Christ and I no longer live, but Christ lives in me. The life I live in the body, I live by faith in the Son of God, who loved me and gave himself for me. (Galatians 2:20)

Application

14 Read 2 Corinthians 5:17 and Galatians 2:20 again.

15 Your new Christian life and freedom depend on
a) your keeping a set of rules.
b) how hard you try to be good.
c) what you know about religion.
d) Christ's presence in you.

You have found in Christ a wonderful new life—eternal life with the glorious freedom of the children of God. Treasure it above all things; you will enjoy it increasingly.

Answers to Application Questions

6 b) trust in the Lord.

1 c) accepting Jesus as your Savior.

7 c) truth we learn in the Bible.

3 b) If you oppose the devil, he will go away from you.

9 b) time of Moses until the time of Christ on earth.

4 a) 1) Freedom now and in the future
  b) 2) Freedom in the future
  c) 1) Freedom now and in the future
  d) 1) Freedom now and in the future
  e) 2) Freedom in the future

10 Statements **a)** and **c)** are true.

5 God allows temptations so you can learn how to overcome them and become stronger.

15 d) Christ's presence in you.

CONGRATULATIONS

You have now completed all the unit lessons. We hope that it has been a great help to you. Review the lessons in Unit Two and complete the *Unit Two Evaluation*. When you have completed the evaluation, check your answers using the answer key in the back of this book.

Officially enrolled students should refer to the *Final Exam Instructions* page following the unit evaluation answer key for directions on taking the final exam.

CL1110 Your New Life

UNIT EVALUATIONS

Directions

When you have completed your study of each unit, complete the evaluation for that unit, and check your answers using the answer key in the back of this book.

Read each question carefully. There is one best answer for each question. Circle the answer you have chosen.

Example

1 To be born again means to
    a) be young in age.
    b) accept Jesus as Savior.
    c) start a new year.

Unit One Evaluation

1. You began a new life
   a) when you decided to become a better person.
   b) the moment you accepted Jesus Christ as your Savior.
   c) after you understood everything about being a Christian.

2. You develop your new nature as a Christian primarily by
   a) trying hard to be like Jesus.
   b) acting like other Christians.
   c) having a daily relationship with Christ.

3. In your new life, God is with you as a
   a) far-off being.
   b) loving Father.
   c) demanding taskmaster.

4. The way to learn how to walk in your new life with Christ is to
   a) feel confident in yourself and your ability.
   b) depend on God and trust Him to help you.
   c) wait until you know everything that you should do.

5. Your heavenly Father is much stronger than the devil and
   a) He will be with you to help you.
   b) tries to help you but sometimes He isn't able.
   c) He will never punish anyone, even if punishment is deserved.

6. To *repent* means to
   a) confess all your sins to a priest.
   b) tell people that you want to change.
   c) be sorry for your sins and turn away from sinning.

7. You can expect God to talk to you because He
   a) made everything that exists.
   b) loves you as your heavenly Father.
   c) is able to do anything He decides to do.

8 God speaks His message to His people by
  a) Christian pastors.
  b) spiritual mediums.
  c) means of witchcraft.

9 The Bible has sixty-six different books and
  a) only one theme.
  b) is hopelessly confusing.
  c) cannot be understood by average Christians.

10 One of the ways to hear God's voice every day is to
  a) ignore everyone else.
  b) believe every thought you have is from God.
  c) make a habit of rereading and memorizing Bible verses.

11 You can find help to grow spiritually by
  a) arguing with others about religion.
  b) performing mysterious religious rituals.
  c) studying the Bible and praying to God.

12 You can overcome discouragement and worry by
  a) depending on your own inner resources.
  b) trying very hard to be happy and not worry.
  c) believing God's promises and depending on Him.

13 A positive way to keep your thoughts pure is to
  a) keep your eyes shut and your ears plugged.
  b) hurt yourself every time you have an impure thought.
  c) focus on pleasing God by obeying the Bible's teaching.

14 One spiritual poison you should keep out of your mind is
  a) hatred.
  b) God's joy.
  c) love for others.

15 The body is strengthened by exercise; the soul is strengthened by
  a) working for God.
  b) worrying for God.
  c) displeasing God.

16 What people do in their free time is usually determined by
   a) their main interests.
   b) other people's opinions.
   c) how much time they have.

17 The different purpose you have as a child of God is to
   a) try to make more money.
   b) enjoy the pleasures of life.
   c) spend time with your heavenly Father.

18 If the pastor says something that offends you, you should
   a) tell others that he or she is not a good pastor.
   b) quit going to church or find another church.
   c) forgive and pray for him or her and keep attending the services.

19 People you see often and to whom you could witness about Jesus include
   a) your family and friends.
   b) celebrities and world leaders.
   c) the spirits of departed loved ones.

20 The most important reason Christians should give offerings is
   a) because they want to become rich.
   b) to act like God who is generous to everyone.
   c) because God punishes those who don't give to their church.

Unit Two Evaluation

1 The standards in a well-ordered home are set by the
   a) parents.
   b) children.
   c) neighbors.

2 The perfect pattern for your new life is found in
   a) your pastor.
   b) Jesus Christ.
   c) the saints of the church.

3 In "The Lord's Prayer," Jesus taught us to pray to
   a) the saints.
   b) our ancestors.
   c) God, our heavenly Father.

4 Jesus teaches us that true success will come if we
   a) try very hard to be happy.
   b) repeat many prayers every day.
   c) base our thoughts, words, and actions on His teachings.

5 God's purpose in sending the Holy Spirit is to
   a) be everywhere at once.
   b) take Jesus' place on earth.
   c) live in you, guide you, and help you.

6 The "fruit" of the Holy Spirit means the
   a) spiritual truths we find in the Bible.
   b) good character qualities produced by the Holy Spirit.
   c) people who hear the gospel message of Jesus Christ.

7 The main purpose of the baptism in the Holy Spirit is to give Christians power to
   a) witness effectively.
   b) earn their salvation.
   c) do miracles of healing.

8 A gift of the Holy Spirit is a
  a) special spiritual present church leaders give.
  b) spiritual ability anyone can have by giving money to the church.
  c) spiritual ability the Holy Spirit gives someone to use for the benefit of all.

9 Your life can be a light because you
  a) are talented with brilliant ideas.
  b) have the presence of Jesus in you.
  c) attend the meetings of the local church.

10 God has placed you where you are so you can be
  a) a light to those in darkness.
  b) fearful but hope for a better future.
  c) less discouraging than your friends might be.

11 Your life can show those around you
  a) how to be happy.
  b) how to be angry and sad.
  c) the way to the Savior and heaven.

12 Many are convinced of the gospel's power because of the changed
  a) talk of those who become Christians.
  b) clothing of those who become Christians.
  c) income amounts of those who become Christians.

13 Christians having a hard time quitting bad habits should
  a) ask for special prayer.
  b) give up going to church.
  c) practice the habits in secret.

14 If your family members don't become Christians immediately, you should
  a) stop praying for them.
  b) keep praying for them.
  c) think that God won't save them.

15 Your home will be happier if you
  a) ask forgiveness when you wrong someone in your family.
  b) show your family you are boss and make them afraid of you.
  c) make family members who wrong you ask for your forgiveness.

16 Couples who keep their marriage vows
  a) have boring love lives.
  b) are not aware of modern realities.
  c) enjoy the blessing of mutual trust and reflect the joy of heaven.

17 You are set free from the guilt, punishment, and power of sin by
  a) deciding to be good.
  b) doing penance for your sins.
  c) accepting Jesus as your Savior.

18 If you aren't delivered immediately from bad habits that tempt you to sin, you should
  a) expect always to have that bad habit.
  b) try to trade the bad habit for a different bad habit.
  c) keep praying and believing God will give you the victory

19 The best way to be free from fear is to
  a) use strong magic.
  b) trust in the Lord's help.
  c) light candles to an image.

20 Your new Christian life and freedom depend on
  a) Christ's presence in you.
  b) your keeping a set of rules.
  c) how hard you try to be good.

Your New Life

CL1110 Your New Life

UNIT EVALUATION ANSWER KEY

Directions

When you have completed a unit evaluation, check your answers using this answer key.

In this key, each question and correct answer is listed, followed by where each correct answer can be found. For example, in the answer below 1.1 indicates that the correct answer is found in Lesson 1, Goal 1.

	Goal
1 c) Correct answer.	1.1

Make note of questions you answered incorrectly, and review the lesson material for those questions.

Unit One

		Goal
1	b) the moment you accepted Jesus Christ as your Savior.	1.1
2	c) having a daily relationship with Christ.	1.2
3	b) loving Father.	1.3
4	b) depend on God and trust Him to help you.	2.1
5	a) He will be with you to help you.	2.2
6	c) be sorry for your sins and turn away from sinning.	2.3
7	b) loves you as your heavenly Father.	3.1
8	a) Christian pastors.	3.2
9	a) only one theme.	3.3
10	c) make a habit of rereading and memorizing Bible verses.	3.4
11	c) studying the Bible and praying to God.	4.1
12	c) believing God's promises and depending on Him.	4.2
13	c) focus on pleasing God by obeying the Bible's teaching.	4.3
14	a) hatred.	4.3
15	a) working for God.	4.4
16	a) their main interests.	5.1
17	c) spend time with your heavenly Father.	5.1
18	c) forgive and pray for him or her and keep attending the services.	5.2
19	a) your family and friends.	5.3
20	b) to act like God who is generous to everyone.	5.4

Unit Evaluation Answer Key 143

Unit Two

		Goal
1	a) parents.	6.1
2	b) Jesus Christ.	6.2
3	c) God, our heavenly Father.	6.3
4	c) base our thoughts, words, and actions on His teachings.	6.4
5	c) live in you, guide you, and help you.	7.1
6	b) good character qualities produced by the Holy Spirit.	7.2
7	a) witness effectively.	7.4
8	c) spiritual ability the Holy Spirit gives someone to use for the benefit of all.	7.5
9	b) have the presence of Jesus in you.	8.1
10	a) a light to those in darkness.	8.1
11	c) the way to the Savior and heaven.	8.1
12	a) talk of those who become Christians.	8.2
13	a) ask for special prayer.	8.2
14	b) keep praying for them.	9.1
15	a) ask forgiveness when you wrong someone in your family.	9.2
16	c) enjoy the blessing of mutual trust and reflect the joy of heaven.	9.3
17	c) accepting Jesus as your Savior.	10.1
18	c) keep praying and believing God will give you the victory.	10.1
19	b) trust in the Lord's help.	10.1
20	a) Christ's presence in you.	10.1

Dear Student,

We hope this study has made you think about your relationship with God. After studying the lessons and answering all the questions, have you wondered, "Am I really a Christian? Do I know God? Is He real in my life?" We want to give you the opportunity now to have a relationship with God.

We have all done wrong things. We have hurt ourselves and others. The Bible calls that sin and we are all guilty: "All have sinned and fall short of the glory of God" (Romans 3:23). Our sin keeps us from knowing God as a loving Father. But God loves us in spite of our sin. He loves us so much He sent His Son to die for us. "God so loved the world that he gave his one and only Son, that whoever believes in him shall not perish but have eternal life." (John 3:16). When He died, Jesus took the punishment we deserved for our sins.

Do you want to make sure Jesus is your Savior? It is simple:

- Admit that you are a needy sinner separated from God, and ask Him to forgive you.

- Believe in Jesus with all your heart, and let Him know you accept Him as your Savior.

You can talk to God in your own words by saying a prayer like this:

Dear Jesus, I know I am a sinner. Please forgive me. I believe You are the eternal Son of God. Thank You for dying on the cross for my sins. Come into my life. Make yourself real in my life. Be Lord of my life today. Thank You for saving me.

If you prayed this prayer and meant it with all your heart, your sins are forgiven and you have eternal life. Jesus is Lord of your life. The Bible says, "If we confess our sins, he is faithful and just and will forgive us our sins and purify us from all unrighteousness" (1 John 1:9).

STUDENT QUESTIONNAIRE

> Please read and fill out the questionnaire on the following page and submit it whether you are studying as a enrolled student or simply for personal enrichment. God bless you as your journey of faith continues!

Student Questionnaire

Your Name ....

Address ....

....

Email ....

Phone (optional) ....

1 Did you pray to accept Jesus Christ as your Lord and Savior for the first time while taking this course?

☐ **yes**   ☐ **no**

If yes, please share your story ....

....

....

....

2 Did this course help you lead someone else to Christ?

☐ **yes**   ☐ **no**

3 Did this course help strengthen you as a Christian?

☐ **yes**   ☐ **no**

If yes, how? ....

....

....

4 Would you recommend this course to someone else?

☐ **yes**   ☐ **no**

Please give us your friend's information and we will contact them about how they can study these materials.

Friend's Name ....

Address ....

....

Email ....

Phone (optional) ....

Cut this page and mail to the International Office USA, or scan and email to sed@globaluniversity.edu

FINAL EXAM INSTRUCTIONS

OFFICIALLY ENROLLED STUDENTS ONLY

- Review all course objectives, application questions, self-tests, and unit evaluations in preparation for the final exam.
- Complete the final exam online using your student number and password at http://sed.globalutraining.com.
- Outside the USA, please submit your final exam and student questionnaire to your instructor or national office.

> Now that you have finished your study of this course we encourage you to begin the next course in this series or ask your instructor to recommend another course of study.